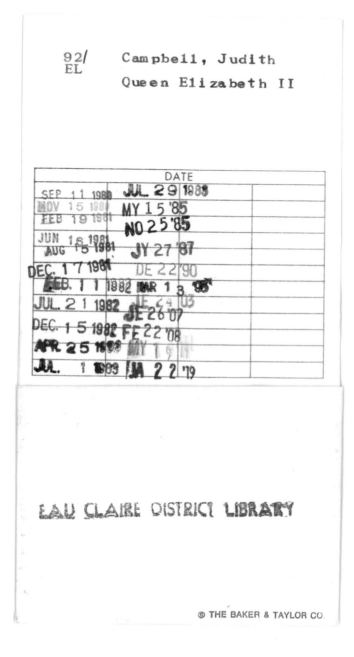

Endpapers *The Queen and Prince Philip riding in the magnificent gold state coach to St Paul's Cathedral for the Silver Jubilee Thanksgiving Service, June 1977.*

Queen Elizabeth II

*After the annual ceremony of Trooping the Colour the Queen pats her mare Burmese,
who was presented by the Royal Canadian Mounted Police and acts as both military charger
and favourite pleasure-riding horse.*

Judith Campbell

QUEEN ELIZABETH II

A Biography

Crown Publishers, Inc., New York

First English edition published by Artus Books Ltd, 1979
Copyright © MCMLXXIX by Artus Books Ltd

First published in the United States 1980 by
Crown Publishers, Inc. by arrangement
with Weidenfeld (Publishers) Limited.

Printed in Italy by L.E.G.O., Vicenza

Library of Congress Cataloging in Publication Data

Campbell, Judith.
Queen Elizabeth II.

1. Elizabeth II, Queen of Great Britain, 1926–
2. Great Britain – History – George VI, 1936–1952.
3. Great Britain – History – Elizabeth II, 1952–
4. Monarchy, British.   5. Great Britain – Kings and
rulers – Biography.
DA590.C249   1980   941.085'092'4 [B]   79-16592
ISBN 0-517-53974-8

Contents

Foreword

'Elizabeth II, by the Grace of God of the United Kingdom of Great Britain and Northern Ireland and of her other Realms and Territories, Queen, Head of the Commonwealth and Defender of the Faith' comes of a dynasty that is rooted in a very remote period of English history. The line of succession spans more than eleven hundred years since Egbert of Wessex was acknowledged the first king of all England and Elizabeth is the seventh queen regnant in that period (that is, a queen in her own right).

The unfortunate, uncrowned Lady Jane Grey was the first queen regnant, but her 'reign' lasted only nine days, and she later paid with her head for her pretension – though she had been nothing but a pawn in the hand of her ambitious father-in-law the Duke of Northumberland. Next came Mary Tudor, the elder daughter of Henry VIII, who succeeded in 1553 after dethroning Jane Grey. Mary was the most unpopular of English queens. She persecuted those of her subjects who resisted her attempts to restore to the country the Catholic Church which her father had overthrown. Mary married King Philip II of Spain (another unpopular move), but the marriage was childless, so she was succeeded by her half-sister, Elizabeth. Elizabeth I was the greatest of the Tudors and, indeed, one of the greatest English sovereigns of all time. She was a shrewd, courageous and inspired sovereign who won the hearts of her people by sheer force of character.

Upon the death of Elizabeth in 1603, the English crown was united with that of Scotland. There had been two Scottish queens regnant. First there was the child Queen Margaret, who reigned only four years, 1286–90, and in fact never set foot in her kingdom. Then there was Mary, Queen of Scots, another child queen who succeeded to the throne when she was only a few days old. Her reign was marked by political and religious ferment, conspiracies and civil war, and her overthrow was followed by a long period of imprisonment in England before her death on the block in 1587.

Eighty-six years were to pass between the death of Elizabeth I and the reign of the next queen regnant, Mary II. But Mary was crowned jointly with her husband, William III, in 1689 and never ruled alone, as she predeceased him. She too was childless, so when William died in 1702, her sister Anne succeeded him. The reign

Opposite *Queen Elizabeth II, the seventh queen regnant, pictured during her state visit to Finland.*

The Queen and Prince Philip – a happy and successful partnership.

of Queen Anne saw the enactment of a formal union between England and Scotland.

Of all the former queens regnant the one whom Elizabeth II admires most, and the one to whom she feels most akin, is her great–great–grandmother, Queen Victoria. And although Victoria is generally remembered as a very old woman, the venerable matriarch of Europe, in her younger days she had many similarities to the present Queen. The young Victoria was lively and intrepid, a lover of open-air life and especially of Scotland's Highlands; and like Elizabeth II, she made a most helpful and rewarding partnership in marriage.

During Victoria's reign wealth from trade and industry made Britain probably the world's most powerful nation; her Empire was the envy of other monarchs. But if Victoria, and the previous queens of England would deplore the diminution of their country's greatness in modern times, blown away by fierce winds of change, there is still much in the career of Elizabeth II that they would admire. The modern British monarchy has accommodated demands of 'power for the people', losing on the way authority and prerogatives cherished by past monarchs, but it has retained a dignity which commands respect, a dedication which cannot be denied and it maintains an example of Christian family life which is a stable base in a world of changing values. Queen Elizabeth II is a down-to-earth, hardworking woman who has gracefully accepted her changing role as sovereign of Britain in the second half of the twentieth century and maintains a successful balance between her public and private life.

Opposite Elizabeth's illustrious predecessors, the previous six queens regnant: Lady Jane Grey, Mary I (Mary Tudor), Elizabeth I, Mary II (who reigned jointly with William III), Queen Anne and Victoria.

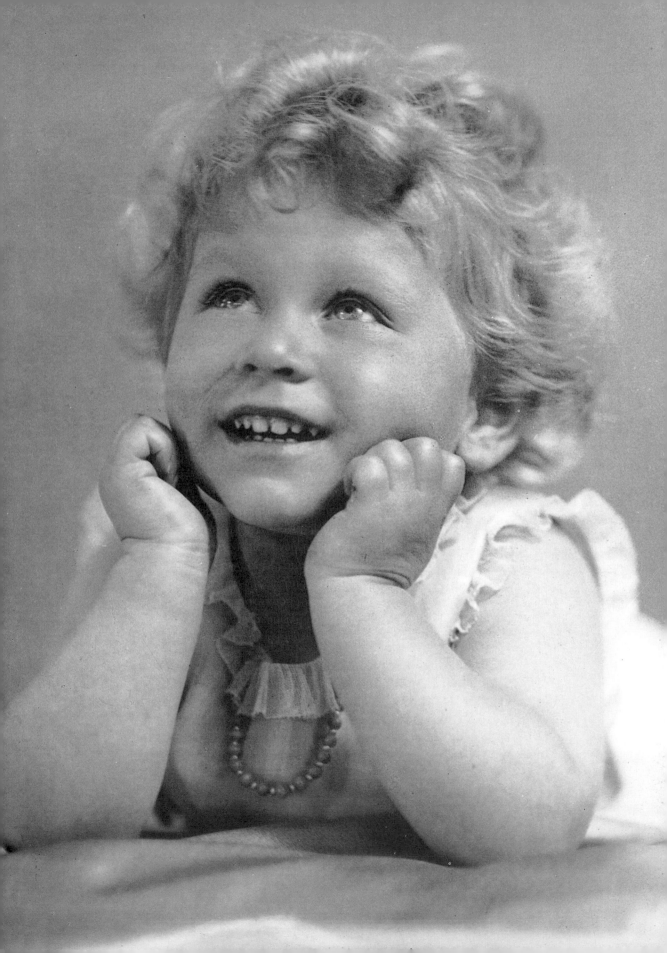

1

The Early Years

Elizabeth Alexandra Mary, the first child of Prince Albert and Elizabeth, Duke and Duchess of York, was born on 21 April 1926. The arrival of this longed-for baby was a joy to her parents and a very happy event in the Royal Family, but there was no great reason for regarding the birth as one of national significance. There was even less reason for surmising that the little girl might one day become Queen.

Elizabeth's father, called 'Bertie' by his family, was the second son of King George V and Queen Mary and second in line to the throne. At birth Elizabeth was therefore third in the line of succession. Although her eldest uncle, the Prince of Wales, was still unmarried at twenty-seven, there seemed every reason to believe that he would marry eventually and have children – who would, of course, supercede their cousin Elizabeth in royal precedence. And if, as also seemed very likely, the Duke and Duchess of York later had a son, he would automatically have prior claim to the throne over any daughters. So, although, like all royal babies, from the moment she was born Elizabeth was *news*, in the beginning public interest was chiefly due to the popularity of her mother, Elizabeth Bowes-Lyon, affectionately known as 'the little Duchess'.

The Duke, though slightly more in the limelight since his marriage and much respected for the conscientious way he carried out royal duties, was quiet and shy and hampered by a distressing stammer. Not only in young adulthood but also in childhood he had tended to be overshadowed by his elder brother's easy, instinctive charm, and his upbringing had done nothing to bolster someone who by nature lacked self-confidence.

Bertie's father, the good-hearted King George V, was a man who had genuinely wished to give his family a happy childhood such as the one he had himself enjoyed, but he had proved to be an excessively stern father, particularly for the sensitive Bertie. Until 1892 (when he became second in line to the throne on the death of his elder brother, the Duke of Clarence), George had made a career in the Royal Navy, and that five-year training in the senior service had strengthened his inborn sense of duty, his orderliness and addiction to work. Added to his natural courage and commonsense, these were virtues that were to stand him in excellent stead during the terrible years of the First World War, which broke out four years after he

Opposite Princess Elizabeth, aged two, the golden-haired, blue-eyed daughter of the Duke and Duchess of York, who few suspected would one day be Queen of England.

became king. They were also traits that endeared him to his people as the model of a conscientious constitutional monarch, one who seemed to embody all that was best in the British character. Unfortunately such admirable virtues did not necessarily make him the easiest of fathers to a young family. Undoubtedly he loved his children, but he was inclined to treat them as a naval officer would noisy midshipmen, as 'young nuisances in constant need of correction'. His bluff, quarter-deck ideas of discipline made him appear unapproachable and when he was in a jovial mood, it inspired a heavy-handed chaffing that his sons did not understand. His manner created a rift between himself and his sons that remained largely unbridgeable until some years after they were grown up.

The children's mother, Princess May of Teck, who became Britain's much loved and respected Queen Mary, was devoted to her family and took great pride in all they did, and although she backed up their father in matters of discipline, she did intercede if she thought he was being too severe. But the Queen was not able to communicate or show her affections easily.

Inevitably both parents subscribed to contemporary nursery-regimented methods of bringing up a family – not the best atmosphere for a highly strung, ultra-sensitive child such as Prince Bertie. To make matters worse, he was for some years in the charge of a neurotic nurse, and when he was seven an attempt was made to 'cure' him of left-handedness by forcing him to write with his right hand. Add to this the painful leg-splints in which Bertie had to sleep as a cure for an inherited tendency to knock-knees, and it is scarcely surprising that he developed the frustrating speech problem that was to dog him for so many years.

In 1909 Prince Bertie, then aged fourteen, began his career as a cadet at the Royal Naval College at Osborne on the Isle of Wight. In due course he went on to Dartmouth, leaving when he was eighteen to join his first ship. As a Sub-Lieutenant in *HMS Collingwood* he was at the battle of Jutland, the principal naval engagement of the Great War, but he spent most of the war years in hospital, first with appendicitis, then with a crippling duodenal ulcer, a legacy of his stressful childhood. In 1916 he transferred from the Navy for a three-year stint with the Royal Air Force then, after the War, aged nearly twenty-four, went up to Cambridge for a year.

The stammer was no better. When relaxed, the Prince could talk with moderate ease. In public, or at any time when he was tense, the affliction could leave him gulping for words in painfully embarrassing pauses. In character he was sincere and unassuming, and he was an above-average sportsman; with those who knew him well enough to penetrate his reserve, he could be a happy, lively companion, despite the bouts of depression from which, scarcely surprisingly, he had always suffered.

Opposite Elizabeth at the age of four weeks, with her mother the Duchess of York, in May 1926. The birth of their first child, Elizabeth, was the greatest joy to the Duke and Duchess of York but they had no inkling of what the future held in store.

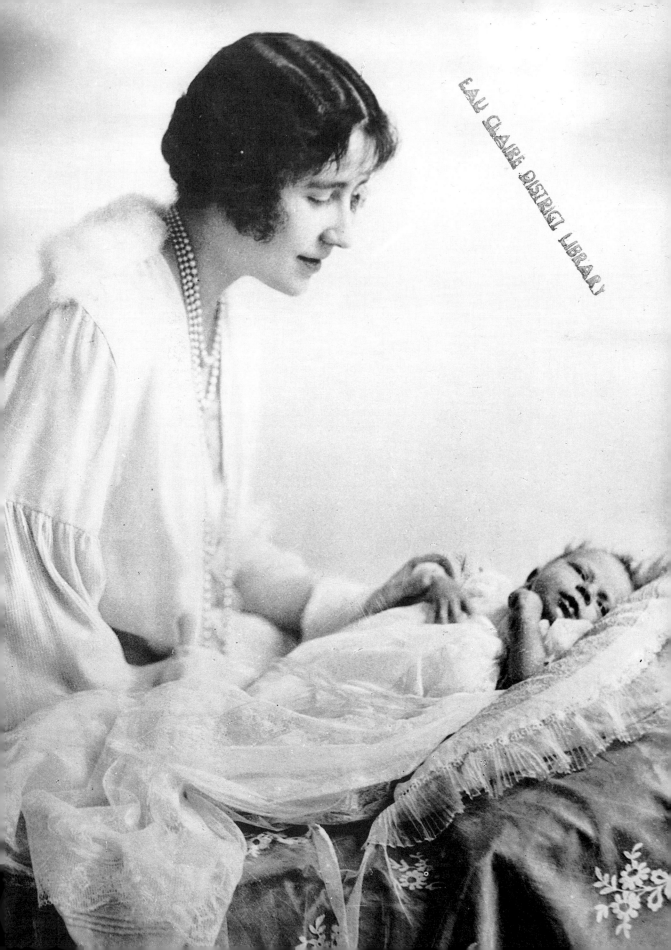

Glamis Castle – visited by Mary Queen of Scots and chosen by Shakespeare as the setting for 'Macbeth' – was the home of the Strathmores, the Queen's maternal grandparents, and holds many happy memories for her.

But, still outshone by the magnetic personality of his elder brother David (titled Edward, Prince of Wales), by 1920, when he was created Duke of York, the King's second son appeared a diffident, self-conscious young man. What few suspected were the reserves of fortitude and persistence that, strengthened by his future wife's loving encouragement, would serve him so well in the difficult years to come.

The Duke first met Elizabeth Bowes-Lyon in 1920. She was the second youngest of the fourteenth Earl of Strathmore's ten children, a country girl brought up in the family's lovely rambling home, St Paul's Walden Bury, in Hertfordshire, and at medieval Glamis Castle in Scotland, to which the family migrated each August. She grew up as a member of a happy, close-knit, boisterous family, educated first by her mother, a lady of many talents, and then by governesses. She was fourteen when the First World War broke out and spent much of her spare time during the next few years helping her mother look after and amuse the war-wounded for whom Glamis Castle had been turned into a convalescent home. When her mother became ill, she took charge of the household.

Lady Elizabeth was barely twenty when the Duke of York, a friend of her brother's, first met her and soon fell deeply in love with her. This girl with the eloquent, strikingly blue eyes, was as unlike the chain-smoking, cocktail-drinking upper-crust girls of the 'fast set' who were included in the Prince of Wales' circle in the 1920s, as the quiet unassuming Bertie was unlike his glamorous elder brother. But Lady Elizabeth's sparkling vitality, her combination of sincerity, kindness and natural gaiety, proved irresistible to men: she had many suitors besides the King's son. Nor was the prospect of her becoming a royal duchess alluring in itself: in fact, the thought of exchanging the independence and privacy of her life for restrictions and publicity, inevitable as a member of the Royal Family, was one of the chief reasons for Lady Elizabeth's refusing the Duke of York's proposal of marriage in the spring of 1921.

The King had always thought Bertie would be 'a lucky fellow' if he were accepted. Lady Strathmore, who liked the Duke very much, hoped he would eventually find a nice wife who would make him happy. Everyone assumed that that was that. But they reckoned without Prince Bertie. Quietly, persistently, he continued to court Elizabeth, although the going was not always easy. But, unlike many, he shared her ideas of emotional fidelity and agreed with the high ideals that governed her life. And in the end the shy, inarticulate young man won the girl who had filled his heart and thoughts almost from the first moment he set eyes on her, and who continued to fill them to the end of his life.

They were married in Westminster Abbey on 26 April 1923. Naturally enough, when the bridegroom is a royal duke, there is no thought that his bride should be married from her own home. Glamis and St Paul's Walden Bury were far too far from the centre of the nation's life for that to be feasible. As it was, there were many members of the enormous Royal Family (including the Dowager Tsarina of Russia) who must be found places at the ceremony, as well as the many dignitaries from Britain and her Empire; and a crowd of over a million people lined the streets to see the bridal procession pass. It was said at the time that such cheering had not been heard since that day in 1918 when the Armistice was signed.

Accustomed as she had always been to the duties of '*noblesse oblige*' in her Scottish home, the new Duchess now had to cope with the many formal engagements that fell to her as a member of the Royal Family. She quickly perceived, however, that her main task would be to support her husband, bolstering his self-confidence and soothing his fears of inadequacy.

The Yorks passed the first months of their married life at their country house, White Lodge, in Richmond Park, then moved to 145 Piccadilly. But when, in the autumn of 1925, the Duchess found that she was expecting her first child, the couple realized that neither home was convenient for the event. So the future Queen Elizabeth II was born (by Caesarian section) at 17 Bruton Street, the Strathmores' London house. The Yorks had longed for a child to make their happiness complete, and as the Duke wrote to his mother it was 'a tremendous joy' to have their little girl. The King and Queen wasted no time in coming to see their first grand-daughter, a pretty baby with fair hair and 'large dark-lashed eyes and tiny ears', and Queen Mary found her 'enchanting'.

When the baby was four months old, she went with her parents and devoted nannie Clara – a name she would soon interpret as 'Alla' – to Scotland, for the annual summer holiday north of the border inaugurated by Queen Victoria, which

Above Baby Elizabeth with her proud parents. A happy family life was the keynote to Elizabeth's childhood.

Right Baby Elizabeth with her grandmother, the Countess of Strathmore, just before leaving Bruton Street to go and stay with the King and Queen at Buckingham Palace.

(apart from the interruption of war and some curtailments by Edward VIII) is one of the traditions continued since that time by the Royal Family. The Duke and Duchess of York did not, however, stay at royal Balmoral but with the Strathmores at Glamis Castle, an innovation they had been enjoying since their marriage and which became an annual event of Elizabeth's early childhood, so that from the start she was introduced to an informal way of life that bore small resemblance to that of her royal grandparents. It was a way of life that had opened up new worlds to the Duke of York in the days when, a nervous, introspective young man, he had escaped the rigid formality of Balmoral and driven north to the castle in the glen of Strathmore. The Bowes-Lyon family was so large that the castle always seemed full of life and noise even without the house-parties that arrived once the London 'season' ended, and the friends who drove in from the surrounding countryside. There were always crowds of lively young people around to play cricket or tennis, to shoot game, dance, act charades or sing round the piano to Lady Strathmore's spirited accompaniment.

The Strathmores' life-style had been moulded by baby Elizabeth's maternal grandmother. Nothing ruffled Lady Strathmore, and she took life in her stride. Unaffected, commanding and at the same time considerate, a devout Christian but without bigotry, she saw to it that family and friends conformed to the ideas of integrity, simplicity and concern for others whose virtues and joys she never questioned. It was an attitude that could have resulted in a formal code of existence as rigid in its own way as that of the King and Queen: in practice it created an exceptionally happy family, with the children, at whatever age, sharing an affectionate, unconstrained relationship with their parents that amazed the Duke of York as much as he envied it. The gaiety, the family jokes, the general freedom of expression that permeated the Strathmore homes were a revelation to a man whose own family life had been so inhibited. And from this grew the happy, loving atmosphere in which his own children were to be brought up.

In October 1926, when Elizabeth was six months old, something occurred that was to affect the Duke's entire future, and through him that of his family and, later, that of the nation: the King decided that it would help 'bring out' his second son to send him, as his representative, to Australia for the formal transference of the federal capital to Canberra. In many ways this was a compliment, an acknowledgement of the conscientious manner in which the Duke carried out his public duties, and he knew he ought to be gratified by his father's suggesting him for such an important mission. Equally he knew the tremendous enthusiasm with which the Australians had greeted his elder brother's 1920 tour and that they were expecting the charming, popular Prince of Wales to return for such a notable ceremony in the country's history. Whether the Duke was also aware that the Australian Prime Minister was said to be 'appalled' by the King's decision, is not known, but when he thought of the speeches inevitably involved with such an occasion, it was a sentiment he fully shared. In conversation at home and with friends his stammer scarcely troubled him now, but in public it was no better at all, and even the most trivial 'public utterance' was difficult.

Desperate at the thought of the little time left before his ordeal, the Duke agreed to see another speech-therapist, Lionel Logue, of whose methods the Duchess had heard a good report. The first meeting took place on 19 October, and from it the Duke emerged with new hope.

Between then and 6 January 1927, when the Yorks embarked in the battle-cruiser *Renown* for their Antipodean tour, almost daily sessions of the new therapy were fitted in. The Duchess also learned the breathing exercises suggested by Logue, so that she could help her husband to continue them while they were away, and although a lifetime of talking the wrong way could not be cured completely in a few weeks, the immediate improvement inspired the Duke with such confidence in the eventual result that the royal tour and the speech-making were a great success. Soon the ability to express himself clearly in public, and at last to his father, altered the Duke's entire outlook, contributing a great deal to both his own happiness and that of his family.

The future king would always retain a slight hesitancy in his speech, especially in moments of stress, and he never came to enjoy public speaking in any form, particularly broadcasting, but, as he was to write after making a fine speech on returning from a Canadian tour in 1939, 'It was a change from the old days when speaking, I felt, was hell!' At the time no one could have realized that the history of the British nation might well have been changed if a cure had not been found for the speech impediment of its future king. No monarch would ever be more reluctant to take up the burden of the crown than King George VI, and if he had still not been able to express himself, he might have found the task physically and emotionally beyond him.

The Australian tour meant that the Duke and Duchess were to be overseas for six months, and it was a hard wrench to leave their baby for such a long time. But this kind of family parting is one of the penalties of being royal: duty has to come before personal inclination – that was one of the royal rules upheld by George V and drummed into his family from their earliest years. It was a principle that failed to take firm root in his eldest son, but one by which his second son lived.

The separation was hard on Elizabeth's parents, but she was too young to be much affected herself. In the safe and devoted hands of Alla, an old-fashioned nannie who had been the Duchess's own nurse, the nursery routine continued as usual. Responsibility for the baby's over-all welfare was shared by both sets of grandparents, and she was unlikely to suffer from lack of attention! She was taken first to stay with the Strathmores at St Paul's Walden Bury, and then in February 1927 to London to be with the King and Queen at Buckingham Palace. Although the surroundings of the nursery suite at the Palace were different, the daily routine continued unaltered – until after tea. Then, wearing one of the delightful little frilly dresses in which all 'well-born' babies of those days appeared (and on special occasions still do), Elizabeth was carried by Alla along the corridors and past huge state apartments to spend a short time with the King and Queen. And the kindly indulgent grandfather whom, as she grew up, Elizabeth called 'Grandpapa England', was never to give her a hint of the man who had sometimes treated his own children, including her father, with a severity that bordered on harshness.

Much of the King's concept of the life and duties of monarchy were to be adopted by Elizabeth's father, and then adapted by herself. But as a young child she knew George V only as the typical grandparent who, without direct responsibility, thoroughly enjoys spoiling the younger generation. In a different way Queen Mary was to exert as much influence on her grand-daughter as the King and was to take a very active role in her upbringing. The Queen's reticent, shy personality never

Elizabeth's nurse 'Alla' (Mrs Clara Knight) took pride in dressing her in the frills of the times – clothes very different to those which would be worn in the future by her royal charge's own children.

Mary R

Baby Elizabeth
1927.

While Elizabeth's parents were on an official six-month overseas tour of Australia in 1927 her grandmother, Queen Mary, had the opportunity to lavish more attention than ever on her little grand-daughter.

A first view of the crowds that would become part of her life. Elizabeth on the Palace balcony with King George V and Queen Mary, and the Duke and Duchess of York, just returned from overseas.

allowed her to show her feelings and affections very openly, and although she had never been emotionally close to her own children, like the King she found this 'sweet little grand-daughter' a joy. And as 'Lilibet' (Margaret's attempt at the name 'Elizabeth' and one that remains a family name today) grew older, Queen Mary saw to it that she fully appreciated the treasures, material and spiritual, that she considered it the unflagging duty of royalty to guard and maintain.

The Duke and Duchess of York arrived home from their tour on 27 June 1927, with three tons of gifts from Australians for their baby. And after the family reunion, for the first time in her life Lilibet was carried out onto the Palace balcony, for the great crowd massed below to greet her parents and cheer the King and Queen. A little later she was brought out again, this time onto the balcony of her new home, 145 Piccadilly. The house was situated across Green Park, within sight of the Palace windows, and it remained the family's London home until the events of 1936 necessitated their move across the Park.

In those days the public's attitude to royal children was considerably more sentimental and less down-to-earth than it is today. Lilibet's first real public appearance, a golden-haired toddler held up beside Queen Mary, had confirmed her emotional appeal for a great number of people. Here was the fairytale princess of their imagination. The media began to keep a close check on the little girl's progress in walking and talking. She was written about, photographed and commented on, and the style and colour of her dresses, coats and bonnets were copied, immediately to become the 'in thing' to buy in toddler-wear. Whenever she was taken out by car, there were throngs of admirers to 'ooh' and 'aah' at a glimpse of her sitting on her nurse's lap. Sometimes the only way to avoid a gathering crowd that had recognized the royal pram entourage on an excursion into Hyde Park was to take to the faster conveyance of a landau and pair, which, by command of the King, could be summoned from the Royal Mews.

Publicity is an inseparable, and most necessary, part of the public life of adult members of the Royal Family, but what is now called 'legitimate interest' in the Royal Family's private life is an outlook born chiefly of the immediacy of television. Before the present reign there was very little pandering to the public's insatiable interest in what goes on inside Buckingham Palace and the other royal residences. Elizabeth's father, after he became king, was to become better known and closer to 'the common man' than any previous British sovereign, through the dangers and privations of the war years shared with his people. Despite this he held the view, understandable for one whose life is mostly public property, that his family-life was his own affair. And this was a viewpoint to which he and his wife subscribed even more strongly in the days when they were Duke and Duchess of York. They were determined that Princess Elizabeth and any subsequent children should not be spoiled by too much public adulation and should be able to enjoy a normal childhood, as far as possible out of the public eye. Where royalty is concerned, however, that is a wish easier to express than to fulfil.

Lilibet was taught at an early age to wave to people who waved to her, and it may have been quite a while before she realized that other children did not have to do the same – and did not have to curtsey to their grandparents. But the day must have dawned when she did realize that she was 'different', and it says much for the good sense of her parents and the watchful eye of Queen Mary that the knowledge was never allowed to give her a feeling of self-importance. On one occasion, during a performance at the Queen's Hall, the little girl was fidgeting and her grandmother asked if she would like to go home. But Lilibet's precocious suggestion that they could not leave before the end, because 'think of all the people who'll be waiting to see us outside', met with short shrift. Queen Mary immediately instructed a lady-in-waiting to take the Princess out by a back exit and home in a taxi.

In 1928 the King contracted bronchial pneumonia. He was so ill that the Duke of York, who had rented a lodge in Northamptonshire for the hunting season, decided to bring his family straight back to London. The usual family gathering at Sandringham for Christmas was cancelled. Although George V's health was never completely restored, he recovered and on doctors' advice went to Bognor (to be

*King George V with his grand-daughter, Elizabeth of York, at Balmoral in
1928. He was an exacting father to his sons, but proved to be a very
indulgent grandfather.*

rechristened 'Bognor Regis' to commemorate the visit) to convalesce in the good
sea air of the south coast. With him went Lilibet, then aged nearly three, to provide
the company that her grandfather most enjoyed.

Their time together, while the King regained his strength, cemented the bond
between the little girl and her grandparents, and if Queen Mary did occasionally say
'no' to Lilibet, the King took delight in spoiling her shamelessly. When he was well
enough, they used to appear on the sea-front together, the bearded, regal figure
with the small girl beside him, both waving to the crowds who gathered to greet
them.

Back home again at 145 Piccadilly, the nursery routine was much the same as that
in any well-to-do family where a nurse was employed. The Duchess could not
devote as much time to her daughter as Lady Strathmore, for all her commitments,

had been able to give to her. The Yorks' public engagements were increasing, and wherever they were, and particularly in London, life could never match the informality of the Duchess's childhood. But there was no question of Elizabeth's upbringing being relegated entirely to a nurse, however devoted: family life was what the Yorks treasured above everything, and the Duke and Duchess would always see more of their children than most London 'society' parents of the times.

The family was completed in 1930 by the birth of a sister for Lilibet, named Margaret Rose. The Yorks might well have been hoping for a boy, but any such aspirations were forgotten once the baby arrived, and their two little daughters were a constant source of happiness and pride. Despite the four years between them, once Margaret Rose was past the baby stage the sisters seemed to bridge the age-gap and became close companions. One reason for this was their comparative isolation from other children. They saw something of their cousins, the two Harewood boys, sons of Mary, Princess Royal; very occasionally other children might come to tea or accompany them to one of the few annual treats – a pantomime, the Royal Tournament, perhaps the International Horse Show; otherwise, for youthful companionship they relied on each other.

There was no lack of adult company. Before the birth of Margaret Rose, Alla was given the help of an under-nurse, a Scots girl named Margaret MacDonald, soon affectionately nicknamed 'Bobo'. When the new baby arrived, Lilibet came more into Bobo's charge, and so began the close and enduring friendship that remains an important part of the Queen's life today. When the Princess was a girl, Bobo slept in the same room; when she grew up, Bobo became her official dresser, a service she continues and combines with that of utterly discreet confidante and dedicated, forthright friend.

When Elizabeth was six, a governess was found, to be responsible for her daytime activities and to make a gentle start on her education. The Princess had been doing a little reading and French with her mother and was grounded in music, drawing and dancing by the same talented tutor.

Miss Crawford – 'Crawfie' to her employers and pupils alike – quickly became the trusted and esteemed part of the family she was to remain for the next seventeen years. It was very sad, and to the Royal Family inexplicable and unforgivable, that after leaving their employ Crawfie was tempted into writing about her experiences in the royal service. There was nothing derogatory in what she revealed, but it concerned the pattern of everyday life, the details that the Royal Family most rightly consider to be totally their own affair and which make up what private life they can call their own. It was an appalling breach of confidence, and it has never been forgiven.

In those days the daughters of the well-to-do never attended state schools and seldom went to boarding-school, and there was no question whatever of those of royal birth attending any school. Miss Crawford's imaginative teaching, the

Opposite Throughout her life the Queen has posed for a great many artists. This portrait was painted by Edmund Brock in 1931.

methods that matched her own lively, energetic personality, were considered exactly what was required both for Elizabeth, and for Margaret Rose when she was old enough to join in. Through the years Princess Elizabeth's educational curriculum was expanded with the aid of occasional 'outside' teachers, particularly after her father's accession when she became Heiress Presumptive.

Queen Mary saw to it that she had a say in the subjects she considered essential for her grand-daughters' education: Bible-reading, geography (particularly of the Dominions), history and dynastic genealogy. The King asked Crawfie to make sure they wrote 'a decent hand'. The Duke and Duchess were basically more concerned with giving their children a secure, happy childhood than with educating them to any remarkable degree. It did not worry them in the least that anything beyond the elementary stages of mathematics remained as much of a mystery to their elder daughter as it had to themselves when young. They wanted their daughters to be able to take a discerning interest in their country's, and the world's, past history and present annals, to be well read in the kind of books that stand up to time, to have their thinking developed so that, when they grew up, they could hold their own in intelligent conversation without necessarily being 'intellectual'. Later, Elizabeth was given specialized tuition to fit her for a specialized job, but during these early

The royal apartments and sunken gardens at Windsor Castle, which was to become one of the favourite homes of the future Queen.

days it was more important that she and her sister should have a home atmosphere in which their personalities could develop without tension. It was a happy, secure life, and with no thought of any other form of education Elizabeth did not feel limited by the restrictions of learning at home. She was a conscientious child with the ability to work hard and a liking for delving deep into the subjects that interested her – but that did not include arithmetic! It was her good fortune that her mother considered the pleasures of the open air and countryside almost as important as strictly academic subjects.

The Duchess also thought it important that her children should be taught the pleasant social accomplishments that she had learned from her own mother. They should be able to dance, to draw and paint if that appealed, to play the piano sufficiently well to provide amusement, and to sing. Good manners, obedience, thought for others were insisted on, and faults were not over-looked. The King's harmless spoiling of Princess Elizabeth was not repeated at home: there was firmness but no trace of severity, and a lot of fun and laughter.

The Duke was becoming yearly more occupied with industrial relations and involved in the creation of the boys' camps that were his special interest, and since the King's illness all his sons had gradually been taking on more of his public duties, although both the Duke and Duchess already had numerous public engagements on their own account. Nevertheless, all their correspondence, their entertaining, anything connected with their public work, was, as much as possible, undertaken in their own home. And as their children grew older, more time was somehow fitted in to be with them.

In London, there was always the 'good morning' session before lessons started, family luncheon if the Duke and Duchess were free, with time for reading together beforehand, and the tea and bedtime rituals which provided the best fun of the day and were omitted only for an engagement of great importance.

In the country, life was considerably more relaxed, and almost all the time there was spent together as a family. The royal expeditions to Scotland in the summer, to Sandringham for Christmas, to Windsor at weekends, had always been the best parts of the year for everyone. Soon Windsor became more enjoyable than ever.

In line with the royal example during the worst of the national economic crises of the early 1930s, the Duke of York had cut personal expenditure on luxuries, but, directly the depression lifted sufficiently to warrant it, he was able to get on with an exciting family project. This was the renovation of Royal Lodge in Windsor Great Park, which the King had offered the Duke and Duchess as a country residence. The place was more or less a ruin, and a great deal of time, work and money was required to turn it into the kind of home of which they had dreamed. For the Duke and Duchess one of the joys of Royal Lodge was designing and working in the garden, and they and the children spent many enjoyable hours at weekends slashing out tangled undergrowth and building bonfires.

Indeed, it would have been very hard for the future Queen not to become the

The Queen's love of horses began at a very early age. Riding Peggy, the little Shetland that was first of a number of ponies.

countrywoman she is at heart. Her mother had been brought up in the country, and country ways and pet animals were a mutual interest. All her father's instinctive enjoyments were rooted in the countryside and the sports that belong to it. Like his father, the Duke came to love Sandringham after he became King. The big, cosy country house and surrounding estate in Norfolk was a place where he would relax among friends and 'put off the king', talking the universal language of forest and field. Like his father, too, he would greatly enjoy proving his marksmanship at shooting, his favourite sport – though the size of the day's 'bag' would bear little relationship to his over-all enjoyment. That lay with the sights and scents and freedoms of the open air. And again like his father before him, George VI would be another king who would end his days at Sandringham, the home he loved best.

As she grew older Elizabeth became as familiar with the flat open landscape and wide expanses of sky in Norfolk as with the heather carpet and gurgling peaty burns on the 'hill' round Balmoral where the family loved to walk. From her father she learned the ways of hare and grouse, woodcock and wild duck; she became familiar with the lore of the wild red deer and loved to watch for a glimpse of the red

Elizabeth riding her tricycle in the garden of 145 Piccadilly.

squirrels that scamper up and down the trunks of the trees at Balmoral, and for the exciting sight of a golden eagle. Above all, like every member of the present Royal Family, she learned to take and enjoy the countryside as it comes, rain, fine, warm, cold or blowing half a gale.

Windsor soon held a special joy for Elizabeth. In London there were always the family pet dogs and her own budgerigars, but the royal riding-horses were then, as now, kept in the mews at Windsor. In her infancy Elizabeth's favourite toys were a collection of miniature horses that were carefully unsaddled and 'stabled' each night before she went to bed. For her third birthday she was given a real pony, a little Shetland called Peggy on which she was led about the grounds of Windsor. This was the first of a series of much-loved but undistinguished ponies, of various shapes and sizes, with which Lilibet, and soon Margaret as well, spent as much time as possible during their childhood. None of them was a paragon of good looks or breeding or, with few exceptions, particularly well behaved, nor were they vastly expensive (one of the larger animals is recorded as costing forty-five guineas, a very moderate sum even for those days). They included a wayward, obstinate pit-pony

Posing for formal photographs, like this one taken by Marcus Adams in 1931, was to become a part of Elizabeth's life.

called George, presented to the Duke and Duchess when they visited a coal-mine. There was Gem, better behaved but with the thick neck and iron mouth typical of her type. Snowball, a docktailed cob, was bought out of a jaunting-car in Ireland and is remembered chiefly for a tendency to whirl round in circles when so inclined. Graylight was the exception of those early years, a good-looking little Welsh mountain mare with gentle manners.

In those days children were not taught the higher arts of riding in the professional way they are today, although when they were old enough, the Princesses had lessons at intervals from an excellent and well-known instructor. This ensured that Elizabeth, a fearless natural horsewoman, achieved a 'good seat' and hands and a rapport with horses that has always made them go well for her; but she never received the basic dressage and initiation into the skills of jumping that her daughter, Princess Anne, was given. Once past the first stage of being led on foot to give her the 'feel' of a pony, Elizabeth was put in the charge of a family groom. He showed her how to hold the reins, attached a leading-rein – a safety precaution with which she found it difficult to make him dispense – and took her out riding. Before long Elizabeth was able to ride with her father, an accomplished horseman, and as soon as Princess Margaret was old enough, she joined them on their delightful weekend rides in Windsor Park.

It was a happy, ordered life, the Duke's methodical ways, a replica of his father's, offsetting the Duchess's more spontaneous outlook. Blissfully happy in his home life, enjoying public work since his speech defect was no longer a burden, the Duke had no reason to query his father's curious reluctance to give him real responsibilities. When the King was ill in 1928, he had been made a Counsellor of State, one of the members of the Royal Family who represent the Crown when the monarch is absent abroad or incapacitated. In those days there seemed no reason for the Duke to question George V's refusal to allow his second son any further access to affairs of state, but, seen in retrospect, this appears an unfortunately blind omission on the King's part.

For the children it was a sheltered life, and a very secure one: they were not pampered, treats were few, and, considering the circumstances, their existence was simpler and less luxurious than might be supposed, but in very few ways, even in the early years, could it be said that Princess Elizabeth's upbringing was 'ordinary', and the understanding she gleaned of the lives and struggles of the people seen from the windows of her home had largely to be born of imagination.

By 1933 Miss Crawford was including a suitably expurgated and simplified few minutes of 'current affairs' in her elder pupil's weekly time-table, but it is unlikely that the fact of a man called Adolf Hitler's becoming Chancellor of Germany would have been sufficiently interesting to include in a seven-year-old's lessons. Unfortunately few British statesmen thought the matter of sufficient menace to warrant their serious attention. There were fewer yet to listen to Winston Churchill, then a political outcast, crying 'Danger!'

If the Duke and Duchess of York had any ideas, one way or the other, on the impact Hitler might have on the future, they would not have expressed them publicly, because British royalty, then as now, were expected to remain aloof from politics, home-bred or foreign. And in private they were, like most of the Royal Family, trying to ignore, or minimize, a cloud that had appeared on the royal horizon and was threatening to grow bigger and blacker.

2

Abdication of a King

When Princess Elizabeth was a small girl, her favourite visitor, and one of the most frequent, was her dashing uncle David, more formally, Edward, Prince of Wales. He often used to call in for family tea and afterwards required little persuading to join in a boisterous game of 'Snap' or 'Rummy' or 'Racing Demon'. Uncle David was fun, and his niece, as receptive to atmosphere as most children, was well aware that this visitor was 'special' for her parents too and that they enjoyed his company as much as she and Margaret did. But his love of 'going against the rules', which the children found irresistible – such as winking at Lilibet on a public occasion to make her laugh, and giving her a puppy at the tender age of three – did not always meet with parental approval.

The story of the uncrowned king, Edward VIII, has been given several different interpretations. To his followers it remains the love story of all time: the story of the man who gave up a throne for the woman he adored. To the majority it seemed a dereliction of duty, but one that in the end turned out to be entirely for the best. To Queen Mary and the rest of the Royal Family it appeared a shocking, unbelievable breach of the almost sacred office of monarchy. But whatever the true elucidation of the story, Elizabeth's Uncle David was the man who shaped her destiny.

From the time the Prince of Wales first emerged into public life at the end of the First World War, he exercised an extraordinary kind of magic over the thousands of people at home and abroad to whom he quickly became a celebrity. In private, particularly as he grew older, he was said not always to be the paragon of good-humoured charm he appeared to be in public. He could be moody and arrogant, sometimes strangely insensitive to the feelings of others. But by the early 1930s he was still casting the same spell over his brothers that they had succumbed to in childhood, when they had mostly to contrive fun and gaiety for themselves – and David was usually their instigator. As time went by, the Prince of Wales' popularity increased, and if the Duke and Duchess of York could not approve of some facets of his private life, they accepted them as 'just David' – even his *affaires*, which, until the advent of Mrs Simpson, were at least discreet. Like the rest of the Royal Family, the Yorks were most anxious that David should soon get married and, secure in their own happy family life, pitied him that he had nothing comparable.

Opposite *Elizabeth returning to Balmoral from Craithie Church with her Uncle David – Edward, Prince of Wales, the man who shaped her destiny.*

The King had been very proud of the enormous success of the Prince of Wales' official tours to the Dominions and other countries overseas, voyagings that had begun with a Canadian tour in 1919. At the time, people everywhere, drained emotionally and materially by the long, horrifying years of war, were finding that instead of the brave new world for which they had fought, strange new economic forces were whittling away the foundations of their lives. Thus, as the last contingents of Dominion and Colonial troops arrived back home, it seemed to Lloyd George, then Prime Minister, that this was a moment when a visit from the Prince of Wales, to thank them on behalf of the King for their great sacrifices and efforts, would do more good than any number of government conferences. The Prince was a young man, he was already immensely popular and his education and outlook had been widened by his active service in the war, through living under all kinds of conditions with all manner of men.

The King approved the idea and until the Prince's return from the last of his assignments, to Africa and South America in 1925, for much of the time his home was a floating one on board a battle-cruiser that sailed the oceans of the world.

But for all the King's natural pride and pleasure in his eldest son's success in public life, he did not entirely understand or approve the over-strenuous and taxing programme of visits to which the Prince agreed. Nor did the King condone the unprecedented informality of his heir's conduct and the somewhat irreverent humour of his speeches on grave occasions. For many reasons it was inevitable that father and son would not see eye to eye: for all his disciplined upbringing, the Prince of Wales was a product of the free-and-easy post-war years, holding views for which King George V, basically more Victorian than twentieth-century, had very little use or comprehension. The Prince, in many ways as restless and questioning of the old order as the majority of his generation, was already impatient of the punctilious regulation of the King's life; his outlook was at odds with much that his father held dear, whether it concerned the world at large or suitable pastimes.

George V could scarcely have expected the Prince of Wales to confine his evening entertainments to those that satisfied the King himself – work on his stamp album, an occasional game of cards, the formal dinner-parties at Windsor Castle that enlivened Ascot week – but he could neither approve the 'society' parties that the Prince of Wales frequented most evenings during the London season nor understand his son's pleasure in them. To begin with, they were mostly held not at private houses but at venues such as the Embassy Club, a respectable and very expensive nightclub envisaged by the King as a disreputable 'dive', where the entertainment apparently mostly began around 11.10 p.m. which was, without fail the King's bed-time. Since all such parties included young women with short hair and short skirts, American jazz and the dances that went with it (four of the modern trends that the King most disliked), his condemnation was a foregone conclusion.

Despite the mutual if seldom expressed family affection, in almost every way the

Elizabeth, the pride and joy of her grandparents, driving back to Balmoral with the King and Queen after attending morning service at Craithie Church.

Prince of Wales was increasingly wishing to live and think differently from his father. While the King, without actually rejecting 'the new', was doing his best to resist it, his son, despite his exalted position, really belonged to the generation that was doing its utmost to change 'the old order'.

The fact that the heir to the throne showed no signs of marrying was a constant source of anxiety to his parents. The subject of his *affaires* with women was never mentioned, and was one they chose to ignore for as long as it was possible.

The Prince of Wales's relationship with Mrs Dudley Ward, an *affaire* that was accepted unquestioningly in the circles in which they moved, began in 1918 and lasted sixteen years. There were other, fleeting attachments during those years, and a more enduring friendship with Lady Furness, who accompanied the Prince on an African safari in 1928. But the Prince was moderately discreet and, though it is difficult to believe in this age of naked truth and gossip-writers, the Press was even more so. The *affaires* of the Prince of Wales might be common knowledge in London society, but if the women concerned were mentioned in the Press at all, not

Edward and Mrs Simpson, their story a kingdom given up for love. Her uncle's abdication meant that Elizabeth became heiress presumptive.

so much as a hint was published to suggest that they were anything more than conventional friends of the Prince of Wales.

He first met Wallis Warfield Simpson at Melton Mowbray in 1931, during a hunting weekend. The weather was cold and foggy: Mrs Simpson had a wretched cold, and although she and her husband had been included in the houseparty, it was obvious that, unlike the other guests, they were not of the fox-hunting fraternity. (They were Americans, who had lived in London since 1928, the year of their marriage. Wallis, whose family lived in Baltimore, had been married before, in 1916, to a United States Naval Air Officer, whom she divorced in 1927. Ernest Simpson, a New York anglophile, was working in the London office of his father's firm, and he and his wife were enjoying their excursion into the life of London society.) That first encounter was brief, but when Mrs Simpson was

The Duchess of York with her daughters, not long before she was crowned Queen Elizabeth, consort to King George VI. Photograph by Marcus Adams, 1936.

introduced to the Prince, her mocking replies to his perfunctory remarks were sufficiently out of the ordinary to impress him. During the next year or so they met occasionally at dinner-parties, and when Mrs Simpson was presented at Court, the Prince of Wales, standing behind the King and Queen's thrones, was struck by her natural grace and elegance.

During those months the Prince was frequently travelling, but when he was in London cocktails at the Simpson's charming flat soon became more of a lure than family tea at 145 Piccadilly. He found his hostess subtle and elusive, very well informed on the engrossing subjects of the day and refreshingly ready to advance her own ideas. It was not long before the Simpsons were included among the regular weekend guests at Fort Belvedere, the Prince of Wales's country retreat on the edge of Windsor Great Park.

Soon the Prince's customary discretion began to slip. To begin with, the parties that included Ernest and Wallis Simpson usually included Lady Furness as well, but after January 1934, when she had enjoyed the attentions of Prince Aly Khan during a visit to America, while the Prince of Wales's friendship with Wallis Simpson had deepened, Lady Furness began to fade out of the picture. After May 1934, it is said, the Prince of Wales never saw Mrs Dudley Ward again and as the months went by Ernest Simpson was more frequently absent.

On two separate occasions, once when asked directly by the King, the Prince is said to have denied categorically that Mrs Simpson was his mistress. According to his autobiography, this was when he began to form the vague dream that somehow, by some means, he would be able to share his life with her. By the end of that year they were to be seen about openly together, at weekend house-parties, at nightclubs, in private houses and public places. The Prince was obviously being 'bewitched', as his youngest brother, Prince George, described it. But whatever view society took of the *affaire*, however resentful and upset the Royal Family might be, the public at large knew nothing about it.

In those days the attitude of the Press towards the personal life of the Royal Family was very different from today. If the editors of the national Press knew anything of the Prince of Wales's attachment to Mrs Simpson, they held their peace, accepting their own edict that the Royal Family's private life was not publishing material.

To the Royal Family, Wallis Simpson's exact status was almost of less importance than the effect she was having on the Prince of Wales's personality. It was not only Princess Elizabeth who was seeing less and less of her favourite uncle. Prince George, closer to David than his other brothers, and often spending long weekends at the Fort, witnessed the beginning of his friendship with Mrs Simpson and disliked what he saw: it seemed to the family that David had little time to spare for anyone but the woman who appeared to be dominating his mind as well as his heart. If he did call in briefly to see the Duke and Duchess of York, he was preoccupied and as uncommunicative with them as he was with the King and Queen and his younger brothers. But it was the Prince of Wales's attitude towards his everyday royal duties that was causing the most anxiety.

It seems very likely that by 1934 the Prince was growing more than a little tired of his duties, and with the advent of Mrs Simpson he seemed to make little effort to hide his irritation and boredom with his royal engagements. Outside the loyal circle of his associates there was still no whisper of the possible cause, but however discreetly the Press photographs and newsreels were edited, the change was there for all to see. The contrast between the smiling, enthusiastic young Prince of yesterday and the moody man of today could not fail to be noticed. But there was no question of these anxieties filtering through to Princess Elizabeth, and no doubt a suitable explanation was offered for her uncle's infrequent appearances. At the end of that year there came an exciting event that fully occupied her thoughts and was a

Princess Elizabeth, aged five, as chief bridesmaid, at the wedding of Lady May Cambridge. (The immediate background was masked so that the photograph of the little Princess could be used alone.)

welcome relief for the family: the King's youngest son, the good-looking Prince George, later Duke of Kent, was to marry Princess Marina of Greece (the charming and graceful cousin of the future Duke of Edinburgh, who was then aged twelve). After a brief courtship, the wedding was to take place in November, and Princess Elizabeth was to be a bridesmaid.

By 1934 economic recovery was on the way, but in parts of the country, 'the depressed areas', there was still massive unemployment, and the over-all gloom of the preceding years seemed to linger on. For many, a happy occasion such as a romantic royal wedding was just the 'lift' that was needed. For the Royal Family the event provided a splendid excuse to concentrate on family joys instead of family troubles, but even so, there was one episode that could not be ignored. The Prince of Wales insisted that the Simpsons be included among the guests at a pre-wedding ball at Buckingham Palace, and for the first and only time the King and Queen met and spoke to Wallis Simpson. It was a very brief and formal introduction.

For the general public the colourful wedding ceremonial had an added attraction. It was Princess Elizabeth's first appearance in such an important rôle and the youthful dignity and composure with which she played her part captured the popular imagination. Throughout the years the Duke and Duchess of York had been coming more into the limelight. After the Duke of Kent's wedding and

39

The Royal Family entering St Paul's Cathedral for the Silver Jubilee Service of Thanksgiving, 1935. From left to right: the Duke and Duchess of Kent, the Duke and Duchess of York, the Duke of Gloucester, Elizabeth and Margaret of York, the Prince of Wales, Queen Maud of Norway, George V and Queen Mary.

throughout 1935 this interest in the Yorks continued to increase, with much of the emphasis on Princess Elizabeth.

In April 1935 Elizabeth had her ninth birthday. It was the year in which Mussolini launched his pre-meditated attack on Abyssinia, and Hitler adopted conscription in Germany. It was also the year in which King George V celebrated his Silver Jubilee, an event the Queen remembers today as her first State ceremony. The two Princesses drove with their parents through the cheering crowds to the Thanksgiving Service at St Paul's Cathedral, where they sat and watched the King and Queen.

As always, there were those who carped about the expenditure, but Queen Mary was proved right in maintaining that 'the people' needed an opportunity to celebrate and have fun. The resulting surge of loyal affection both at home and in the Dominions astounded the King: George V had a great sense of his position as sovereign, yet, essentially a modest man, it had never occurred to him that his subjects should like him for himself. Yet the King's popularity was chiefly because he was exactly what, according to his eldest son, he called himself: 'a very ordinary fellow'. He was not an intellectual, or particularly talented or witty, but he was British 'to the backbone' and a transparently honest, good man. The people liked the orderly example of the King and Queen's happy life together, their piety and the royal example, which the King felt was so important and secretly dreaded would be lost once he was gone. They liked the personal touch of his Christmas broadcasts, an innovation introduced in his later years that brought the King's words, live, into the homes of everyone who had a 'wireless', creating a warm bond between sovereign and subjects.

In the autumn of 1935 there was another royal wedding. The King's third son, Henry, Duke of Gloucester, married Lady Alice Montagu-Douglas-Scott, daughter of the Duke of Buccleuch, and this time both the young Princesses were bridesmaids. But owing to the death of the bride's father only a short while before, the ceremony became a quiet family affair held in the private chapel at Buckingham Palace.

These royal events, all within twelve months, provided a lot of excitement and interest for Elizabeth and Margaret. Combined with the General Election (which brought the Conservatives headed by Stanley Baldwin into power) – a week after the Gloucester wedding, they were also distractions for the older members of the Royal Family – but each time the relief was only temporary, and as the year wore on, there were new, deeper causes for anxiety in addition to the abiding worry about the Prince of Wales.

The King's health was failing. Increasingly disturbed by the intensifying threat of war in Europe, his strength had been sapped by the functions and ceremonies of the Jubilee. He was only seventy, but physically he had never been quite the same since a serious riding accident when reviewing his troops in France in 1915 had resulted in a badly fractured pelvis. The illness of 1928, when he so nearly died, had left its mark with general weakness and recurring bouts of bronchitis. Then, on the morning that the King was to drive in state to open the new session of Parliament, his favourite sister, Princess Victoria, died. Except when prevented by illness, George V had never before allowed personal considerations to interfere with public duties. On that day he felt he could not face the crowds and long hours of ceremonial. The state ceremony was cancelled, and the King never again appeared in public.

George V's increasing frailty had a far-reaching effect on the Prince of Wales's future. By the spring of 1935 the Prince's vague, compelling dream of somehow being able to marry Wallis Simpson had become obsessive, although he was under no delusions about the difficulties. As he himself later asserted in his autobiography, it was his firm intention to discuss the matter some day with his father, although again he realized just how difficult that would have been. The right moment never came. How could he raise a matter that was sure to distress and outrage his father, bring discord into the family, produce a tempest of opposition from the Establishment and the Church, just when preparations for the King's Jubilee were going forward? Or during the festivities? Or when the King was so fatigued by all the celebrations? Or when the Gloucester wedding was at hand? Least of all when his aunt had just died? And so the matter was not discussed between father and son then or, as it turned out, ever.

It is just possible that the result of such a talk might have been different from what the Prince of Wales expected. It would appear from his autobiography that he himself felt he could not discount the possibility of having to withdraw from the

Below *Elizabeth, with Margaret in the pram, out for a walk in the park with Clara Knight (Alla), pushing the pram, and Margaret MacDonald (Bobo).*

Bottom *Fun and games for the young princesses during a fête in the grounds of Abergeldie Castle, Scotland.*

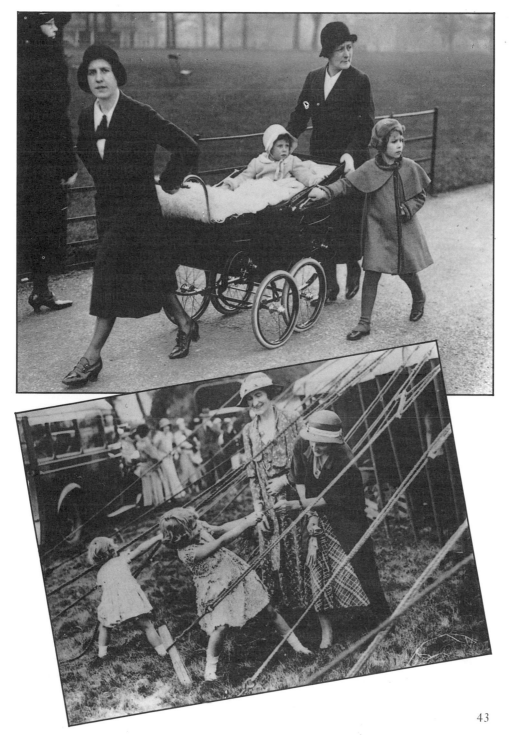

line of succession if he and Wallis married, and that he took comfort in the knowledge that his brother Bertie, the Duke of York, so much more like their father in temperament and outlook, would then succeed to the throne. Although the King would have been shocked and troubled beyond belief, and though there could never have been the remotest possibility of his contemplating Mrs Simpson as a future Queen, George v's reactions to the idea of his eldest son's abrogation of his rights might have been favourable. It would have taken time. The King would have found it inconceivable that any son of his could consider such a dereliction of duty for any reason except ill-health, let alone for the sake of a woman who was already a divorcée and not then in a position to marry. But once convinced beyond all doubt that the Prince intended to make Wallis Simpson his wife when she was free, his father might have been secretly relieved.

The Prince of Wales's behaviour was causing the King more anxiety that year than ever before, and it was not just the way he flaunted his association with Wallis Simpson, or what his family saw as her increasingly ominous influence over him: the Prince was becoming less and less discreet in his utterances in public as well as in private. In June that year, at a British Legion rally in the Albert Hall, he had gone so far as to support an apparent gesture of friendship to Germany – wrongly interpreted by the American and German Press as a reflection of the British government's attitude.

By August (according to Robert Lacey in his book *Majesty*), the King, on holiday in Scotland, was confiding to his friend Cosmo Lang, the Archbishop of Canterbury, that after he was gone he reckoned 'the boy would ruin himself in twelve months'. There is no doubt that the King wished the impossible, that Bertie had precedence over his elder brother, and that he felt that this second son, with his delightful wife, would carry the trust of the monarchy to the best advantage of the nation. How seriously George v considered the matter is not known. Nor is it known if the Duke of York had any inkling of all this, or whether he did know and left an idea that he dreaded buried in the bottom of his mind. (Whether either the Prince of Wales or the King gave any thought to what such an idea would mean to Princess Elizabeth in the years to come, is another unknown factor.) What is obvious is that the Prince's renunciation of his rights, bad enough in itself, would have caused less furore and distress in the long run than abdication, an inconceivable course of action at that time. But the Prince of Wales did not find an opportune moment during the spring, summer or autumn of 1935 to discuss these urgent matters; the King had never been able to start a conversation about Mrs Simpson with his son, and by the Christmas of that year it was too late.

As usual the family gathered at Sandringham for Christmas, but it was hard to put on a show of festive spirit. The King looked thin and frail and was sometimes unfamiliarly vague. All the older members of the family were facing the realization that this was likely to be George v's last Christmas, and they did their best to make it a happy one for him, building it round the nine-year-old Elizabeth romping with

Sandringham House, Norfolk, a cosy, country house in spite of its size became a favourite home for Elizabeth's grandfather and later her father, both of whom died there.

Margaret around the twenty-foot tree in the ballroom. Even the Prince of Wales, preoccupied with his own troubles, conscious that events were rapidly closing in on him, did his best to forget for a while and rallied to join in the children's fun.

Christmas Eve came and went. There were the usual mounds of parcels with presents for the family, staff and estate-workers alike. On Christmas Day Elizabeth and Margaret went with Queen Mary, their parents and their uncles and aunts to the little Sandringham church, close by the Big House, singing carols in that place where the King had so often worshipped through the years, and where he was so soon to lie for a brief while in his coffin before the altar.

The Christmas holiday at Sandringham extended well into January. On the 16th the children were playing outside in the garden when Queen Mary came to tell them that their grandfather was very ill, and later, so it is said, took Elizabeth in to say goodbye. She was a sensible, serious-minded child, and the family were right in thinking her old enough to understand such things. All the same, it must have been a sad, solemn moment for a little girl, and she would hold the memory of the bent, frail figure, sitting wrapped in an old Tibetan dressing-gown, whose kindness and love she had always known and whose influence on her future was to extend so far beyond his own lifetime. Before the end came, she and Margaret were back at Windsor.

King George V died at five minutes before midnight on 20 January 1936.

King Edward VIII following his father's funeral cortège with his brothers Prince Albert, Duke of York, who succeeded him, Prince Henry, Duke of Gloucester and, behind, Prince George, Duke of Kent, who was killed on active service.

His coffin was brought from Sandringham by a bearer-party from the King's Company, 1st Battalion Grenadier Guards, by train to London, to be drawn through the streets on a draped gun-carriage, followed by a simple procession of the Royal Family, for the lying-in-state in Westminster Hall. During the next four days nearly a million people filed past the magnificent catafalque to pay their last tribute to a good king and very honest man, and, whether they realized it or not, to the passing of an era. Because the children were so young the Duchess asked Miss Crawford to minimise the sadness of their grandfather's death as far as was feasible. Margaret was too young anyway to have much understanding. Elizabeth, distressed by the loss of someone she loved who was so much a part of her life, reacted typically for her age. She felt that perhaps she and her sister ought not to play.

Princess Elizabeth had not been included in the family procession through the streets, but she was brought to stand for a few minutes beneath the lofty hammer-beamed roof of what is part of the old Westminster Palace, to watch that silent throng paying their final homage, and to see the dead King's four sons – the new King, Edward VIII, her father the Duke of York, Henry, Duke of Gloucester and George, Duke of Kent – all in full ceremonial uniform standing with heads bowed over their swords, on motionless vigil one at each side of the bier.

Some said that the new King's grief at the death of his father was excessive, that he almost 'went to pieces' at the time, and certainly he had sufficient cause. The expectation of death seldom minimizes the shock when it actually occurs, and although Edward had accepted that his father's days were numbered, he was not alone in finding them dramatically curtailed. He was already tense and troubled almost beyond bearing. Now, in addition to private grief and taking over the tremendous onus of the highest office in the land, he knew that the urgent matter dominating his private life must take a different, even more difficult course.

At once he was caught up in all the constitutional ritual designed to ensure continuity – 'The King is dead. Long live the King.' When the funeral rites were completed, it was time for the new King to take on all the duties, familiar from childhood, but difficult to equate with himself instead of his father.

He quickly learned not to pay much attention to public eulogies from those in high places. Only a short while before King George's death, the Archbishop of Canterbury, at a dinner attended by the Prince of Wales, had made a speech containing glowing references to the Prince and his numerous public services. But the day after the funeral, the Archbishop, at Buckingham Palace to pay his respects to Queen Mary, asked if the new King would receive him, and the conversation boded ominously for their future relationship. Wallis Simpson's name was never mentioned, but it was galling for Edward VIII to discover that the late King had discussed his son's *affaire* with the prelate, and that the Archbishop totally disapproved of the friendship.

The Times lauded the new monarch on his kingly attributes. In a statement to the House of Commons the Prime Minister praised the new King's special qualities, the wide experience he had gained during his years as heir to the throne; he was one who had 'the secret of youth in the prime of age', enthused Mr Baldwin. But privately he was already expressing doubts about the new King's ability to 'stay the course'.

Edward VIII himself, determined now that he was King to be a successful, if modern-day version of a monarch, seemed to be aware that though many looked to this new reign as a happy augury, there was somehow an undercurrent of public unease. It was nothing to do with Mrs Simpson – the British Press was still respecting its self-imposed embargo, and outside the Royal Family and governmental and society circles, her name meant little or nothing. But as his subjects assessed this man now holding the highest office in the land, they were realizing that the self-will and self-indulgence easy to excuse in a young and charming prince denoted, in a forty-one-year-old king, an immaturity that was not assuring.

In those early days the King occupied himself in a flurry of constitutional activity. His public appearances were curtailed by the period of Court mourning, but there was plenty to do, learning routine matters that were now an inescapable part of his daily life, seeing his ministers and officials and the innumerable people who considered they had urgent need to speak with the King. 'The King business' (an equerry's description of the crowded royal diary of engagements) kept him fully occupied. In the first months he was meticulous in reading, and making marginal notes and comments on all the highly confidential and most secret government papers that, contained in the famous red boxes, arrive daily and of right for the monarch's perusal. It was not long, however, before there were few if any notes, and the documents were returned after alarmingly lengthy delays, the majority obviously unread. At weekends the King entertained extensively at Fort Belvedere, and it became apparent that the red boxes were being taken there, and that records of even the most important and top-secret Cabinet discussions were being left unguarded from the possible attentions of the King's cosmopolitan range of guests.

Nor was this all. The international situation was rapidly worsening. March 1936 saw Germany's re-occupation of the Rhineland, a violation by Hitler of the Locarno Treaty that could have meant intervention by Britain, pledged, with Germany and other countries, to keep the Rhineland zone demilitarized. In May Mussolini's invading forces captured Addis Ababa, the capital of Abyssinia, and the League of Nations, advocated by Britain and the USA and created in 1920 to 'settle disputes by arbitration', was attempting, albeit feebly, to enforce sanctions against Italy. That autumn saw the initiation of the Rome-Berlin Axis, which ensured the co-operation of Nazi Germany and Fascist Italy between 1936 and 1945. The Anti-Comintern Pact was signed by Germany and Japan in November. And that was the year when Edward VIII, professing inability to see either Hitler or Mussolini as a threat to British security, was making no secret of the fact that he did not agree with his Government's conduct of British foreign policy. After the war (according to one of the royal biographers, Robert Lacey), evidence apparently emerged to show that Edward VIII had privately assured the Italian ambassador that the League of Nations could be 'considered dead', that 'for peace in Europe it was absolutely essential that two great nations, Germany and Italy, should be afforded full satisfaction by granting them, with full realization of their needs, the necessary colonial markets' – views also apparently expressed to Hitler's foreign minister, and which, whether the dictators misconstrued the limits of a British monarch's powers or not, must have boosted their hopes of keeping Britain neutral.

The King's negligence with confidential documents must be put down to inexcusable carelessness; the more than indiscreet talk could have been due to the same cause, or to the unconscious conceit of a man who reckoned he could be of use to his country by putting his own construction on the role of constitutional monarch. It could perhaps have been due to the King's mental confusion and strain on realizing that he could not carry on without marrying Wallis Simpson, while fully understanding the constitutional impossibility, at that time, of such an action. Whatever the cause and whatever the truth, the Prime Minister dealt at least partly with the situation by limiting the confidential documents sent to the King, to those requiring his signature. And it is a pointer to Edward VIII's state of mind that he never even realized that such a totally unconstitutional act was being perpetrated.

To the Royal Family it seemed that whichever way they looked that year, at home or abroad, the clouds were growing thicker and more ominous. The King was parading his infatuation with Mrs Simpson ever more openly. In the summer of 1936 he began to nullify the reticence of the Press by insisting that Mrs Simpson's

The new issue of postage stamps for the King who was never crowned – Edward VIII.

name be published in the Court Circular among those of prominent guests invited to his dinner-parties. To many this appeared as a method of giving Mrs Simpson a façade of respectability. His family had seen two previous and long-lasting *affaires* (with Mrs Dudley Ward and Lady Furness) eventually fade away, but there seemed no end to this one. And if it did not end soon, what would be the outcome? How much damage had already been done to the monarchy? How much more damaging would it be when, as must happen sooner or later, the King's blatant *affaire* with a married woman became generally known? It is more than probable, if inconsistent, that the family did not even put to themselves, in those early months, the question of what would happen if the King, immovable from his interpretation of where his loyalty lay, should contemplate marriage. For them, the thought would have been inconceivable.

For Princess Elizabeth it was a summer when her grandmother, Queen Mary, stepped up their enjoyable visits together to places of interest in London – historical buildings and museums, anywhere that the Queen felt would instil in her grand-daughter a sense of the grandeur of Britain's past and present, of the nature of the trust the monarchy holds in fief from the nation. Miss Crawford, the governess, took Elizabeth and Margaret about as well, on unobtrusive outings to further their education and for amusement, to such places as the zoo and 'Beckonscot', the model village at Beaconsfield – expeditions that often produced another form of training as well, for the children were usually recognized, a crowd, sometimes including a Press photographer, would gather round, and it became another lesson in accepting publicity as a part of life. Swimming lessons, very popular for sometime, were increased, and Elizabeth began training for her Life-Saving certificate. At home

Above *The Princesses had tremendous fun with 'Y Bwythyn Bach', the miniature cottage in the grounds of Royal Lodge, Windsor, presented to Elizabeth by the people of Wales in 1933.*

Right *The photograph may be posed but the rapport between Elizabeth and her dog is unmistakable.*

Left *Elizabeth taking a morning ride with her father in Windsor Great Park. This picture was taken by special permission on the Princess's tenth birthday.*

there were always the dogs to exercise and play with, ponies to ride at Windsor, and all the fun of 'Y Bwythyn Bach', the miniature cottage presented to the Princesses by the people of Wales, which stood in the grounds of Royal Lodge for them to play in, and where they could practise cooking and keeping house.

The anxieties besetting the Royal Family were deliberately kept from Princess Elizabeth and her sister, but they did meet Mrs Simpson on at least one occasion. The King brought her to Royal Lodge when he drove over in a new American shooting-brake he wanted to show his brother. Tea with the children followed the demonstration, and, according to the 'ghost writer' of the book written for Mrs Simpson after she became Duchess of Windsor, it was 'a pleasant hour'. But that description finishes with the words: '. . . I left with a distinct impression that while the Duke of York was sold on the American station-wagon, the Duchess was not sold on David's other American interest.'

In the autumn of 1936 Wallis Simpson was living in a rented house at Felixstowe, her divorce petition due to be heard on 27 October. The American Press was full of the matter and openly speculating that she would marry the King when she was free. How much longer would British editors remain silent? The King asked his friend Lord Beaverbrook, a power in the newspaper world, if he could help in protecting Mrs Simpson from sensational publicity, and with the help of the Hon. Esmond Harmsworth, another sympathetically inclined newspaper magnate, an unprecedented 'gentleman's agreement' was reached with the other editors. The Simpson divorce proceedings were reported without sensation or implication. (The ultimate scandal of Ernest Simpson's citing the King as co-respondent was averted by Simpson himself providing the necessary evidence of adultery, leaving Mrs Simpson 'the injured party'.) But the heat was on, the pace beginning to quicken.

A few days before the decree nisi came through, the Prime Minister requested an audience with the king. It was a difficult conversation. The rumours and criticisms appearing in the American and Canadian Press were causing Baldwin much anxiety, he said, and could affect the monarchy. The object of the visit, if not stated openly, was then made plain. Would the King persuade Mrs Simpson to drop the divorce proceedings? The King politely declined 'to interfere with the affairs of an individual'. The visit ended without the question about his marriage intentions being asked. But on the evening of 13 November, an urgent letter from his private secretary was handed to the King. In it he was informed that the Prime Minister and Government were meeting to discuss 'the serious situation' which was developing: the Press silence was about to be broken; there was probability of the Government resigning; and the King should know that he would be unable to form a new one. It was imperative that Mrs Simpson go abroad immediately.

When the King told Wallis that 'they' wanted him to give her up, she was apparently as stunned as he had been. Yet they could not have been so naïve as to

Left *An unprecedented and poignant moment in the history of the British monarchy. The ex-King's farewell speech to his people, December 1936.*
Right *The front page of 'The Evening News' on Thursday, 10 December 1936, carried all the bewildering drama of the Abdication. Little Elizabeth appears at the foot of the page, as the new heiress presumptive.*

expect any other reaction to the idea of a twice-divorced woman becoming queen.

There were two more meetings with Stanley Baldwin. During the second one the King told his Prime Minister that he intended to marry Mrs Simpson as soon as she was free; he would remain king if he could, but, if the Government opposed the marriage, then he was prepared to go.

Now it was out in the open, the issue and the word – abdication. And that same night the King went to tell his mother.

During their meal the tension was almost unbearable. Yet, somewhat to his surprise, when he spoke to Queen Mary and his sister Princess Mary of his love for Wallis, a subject that had never before been mentioned between them, they showed the same sympathy that any mother and sister might have done. Nevertheless, when they realized that he was prepared to abdicate rather than give up the woman he put before a throne, it was a point of view that neither was capable of understanding. As Queen Mary was to write to her eldest son two years later, all her life she had put her country before everything else; like the rest of the Royal Family, the Queen could never reconcile her own interpretation of duty to the nation, which if necessary involved sacrifice, with what seemed to her his self-indulgent concept of duty to the woman he loved.

The next morning the King told his brothers that, rather than give up Wallis, he was prepared to abdicate. They too could not believe it. They had all been brought up to the same ideals, and what he was saying went against everything they had been taught and in which they believed. But if the Duke of Gloucester and the Duke of Kent were angry and bewildered, the Duke of York was speechless. It was bad enough that his whole life was to be disrupted, that he was being left to shoulder a burden of which the very thought filled him with dread. But if they had to, he and the Duchess could cope with anything they saw to be their duty; no, this word 'abdication' did not concern only their two selves: it concerned a much-loved ten-year-old daughter, and that was another matter.

LATE NEWS!

Remarkable testimony to YEAST-VITE, the World's Wonder Quick Tonic, pours in. Thousands relieved daily of HEADACHES, NERVES, DEPRESSION, EXHAUSTION, INDIGESTION, INSOMNIA. Don't suffer longer. NO RELIEF NO PAY!

Yeast-Vite

Brand Tablets: Sold Everywhere 2s. 6d., 1.3.3 4s. 6d.

NO. 17,134   FIFTY-SIXTH YEAR

The Evening News

LARGEST EVENING NET SALE IN THE WORLD

BROADCASTING PAGE 6

LONDON : THURSDAY, DECEMBER 10, 1936

LATE EXTRA

ONE PENNY

THE KING ABDICATES

"My Final and Irrevocable Decision": The Duke of York Succeeds To The Throne at Once

"I CAN NO LONGER DISCHARGE MY HEAVY TASK WITH EFFICIENCY"

Abdication Instrument Signed To-day With The Three Royal Brothers as Witnesses

MESSAGE READ TO PARLIAMENT

"My Mind Is Made Up: Further Delay Cannot But Be Most Injurious"

King Edward the Eighth has abdicated his Throne. He announced his decision in the following message which he sent to Parliament this afternoon and which was read by the Speaker to the House of Commons:

The Duke of York.

The Duchess of York.

Their elder daughter, Princess Elizabeth.

After long and anxious consideration I have determined to renounce the Throne to which I succeeded on the death of my Father, and I am now communicating this My final and irrevocable decision.

Realising as I do the gravity of this step, I can only hope that I shall have the understanding of My peoples in the decision I have taken and the reasons which have led me to take it.

I will not enter now into My private feelings, but I would beg that it should be remembered that the burden which constantly rests upon the shoulders of a Sovereign is so heavy that it can only be borne in circumstances different from those in which I now find Myself.

I conceive that I am not overlooking the duty that rests on Me to place in the forefront the public interest, when I declare that I am conscious that I can no longer discharge this heavy task with efficiency or with satisfaction to Myself.

THE ABDICATION INSTRUMENT

I have accordingly this morning executed an Instrument of Abdication in the terms following:

"I, Edward the VIII of Gt. Britain, Ireland and the Dominions beyond the Seas, King, Emperor of India, do hereby declare my irrevocable determination to renounce the Throne for Myself and for my descendants, and My desire that effect should be given to this Instrument of Abdication immediately

"In token whereof I have hereunto set My hand this tenth day of December, nineteen hundred and thirty-six, in the presence of the witnesses whose signatures are subscribed.

(Signed)   Edward R. I."

My execution of this Instrument has been witnessed by My three brothers, Their Royal Highnesses The Duke of York, the Duke of Gloucester and the Duke of Kent.

I deeply appreciate the spirit which has actuated the appeals which have been made to Me to take a different decision, and I have before reaching my final determination most fully pondered over them.

But my mind is made up. Moreover, further delay cannot but be most injurious to the peoples whom I have tried to serve as Prince of Wales and as King and whose future happiness and prosperity are the constant wish of My heart.

I take My leave of them in the confident hope that the course which I have thought it right to follow is that which is best for the stability of the Throne and Empire, and the happiness of My peoples.

"NO DELAY OF ANY KIND"

I am deeply sensible of the consideration which they have always extended to Me, both before and after my accession to the Throne, and which I know they will extend in full measure to My successor.

I am most anxious that there should be no delay of any kind in giving effect to the Instrument which I have executed and that all necessary steps should be taken immediately to secure that my lawful successor, My brother, His Royal Highness the Duke of York, should ascend the Throne.

EDWARD R.I.

The King To Go Abroad

The Press Association learns that King Edward will leave the country immediately after signing his Act of Abdication — probably to-morrow night.

King Edward will renounce with the Throne all his titles. It is probable that the Duke of York will confer a high peerage, probably a dukedom, on him.

King Edward's destination is being kept a close secret. But it is stated on what is described as good authority, that it is not a British Dominion or a British possession.

It is believed that there will be no alteration in the Coronation date fixed for May 12.

Proclamation on Saturday

It is authoritatively stated that the Accession Council will be held on Saturday morning. The new King will be proclaimed on Saturday afternoon.

A change in monarchy is the one occasion upon which all the members of the Privy Council with the Lord Mayor, Aldermen and other representatives of the City are summoned to be present.

New King May Be George VI

It is understood that the Duke of York has not yet made a decision as to what title he will take. It is considered likely that he will choose to be known as George the Sixth rather than Albert the First.

Sensational Speech By Mr. Baldwin

"THE KING SAID: 'I AM GOING TO MARRY MRS. SIMPSON . . . I AM PREPARED TO GO'"

MR. BALDWIN made a sensational speech in the House of Commons after King Edward's message had been read.

Here are points from the speech which is reported fully on **Page Three:**

No more grave message has ever been received by Parliament.

His Majesty, as Prince of Wales, has honoured me with his friendship for many years, which I value.

When we last said good-bye on Tuesday night at Fort Belvedere we both knew and felt and said to each other that that friendship, far from being impaired by the discussions of this last week, bound us more closely together than it ever had and would last for life.

"We Must Settle It"

I felt bound to speak to the King in view of the volume of correspondence which was coming to me in October. I told the King that I wanted to talk it over with him as a friend to see if I could be of help to him.

He said: "You and I must settle this matter together. I will not have anyone else interfering."

I saw him the next time on November 16. I spoke to him on that occasion for twenty minutes on the question of marriage.

I told him that I did not think that a particular marriage was one that would receive the approbation of the country.

I pointed out to him that the position of the King's wife was different from the position of the wife of any other citizen in the country.

"I Am Prepared To Go"

Then His Majesty said to me, and I have his permission to repeat it. He said that he wanted to tell me something that he had long wanted to tell me.

He said: "I am going to marry Mrs. Simpson, and I am prepared to go."

I said: "Sir, that is most grievous news. It is impossible for me to make any comment on that to-day."

He sent for me again on November 21. In the meantime a suggestion had been made to me that a possible compromise might be arranged. The compromise was that the King

should marry and that Parliament should pass an Act enabling the lady to be the King's wife without the position of Queen.

When I saw His Majesty on November 25 he asked me if the proposition had been put before me and I said Yes.

I told him that I had not had a considered opinion, but if he asked me my personal reaction informally, my reaction was that Parliament would never pass the Bill.

Before The Cabinet

I asked him if he desired me to put forward the matter formally. He said he so desired. I told him it would mean my putting it before the whole Cabinet and communicating with the Prime Ministers of the Dominions.

He said that was his wish, and I told him that I would do it.

It is difficult to realise that His Majesty is not a boy. Although he looks so young he is a matured man with great experience of life and of the world.

He wanted to go in circumstances which would make the succession of his brother as little difficult as possible.

He stayed down at Fort Belvedere because he said he was not going to come to London while these things were in dispute because of the cheering crowds.

A Pencil Note

Mr. Baldwin then produced what he said was a pencil note sent to him by the King this morning.

The note said that the Duke of York and the King "have always been on the best of terms as brothers and the King is confident the Duke deserves and will receive the support of the whole Empire."

Continuing, Mr. Baldwin said: "This crisis has arisen now rather than later from that frankness of His Majesty's character which is one of his many attractions."

This evening I shall ask leave to bring in the necessary Bill which will be available to members as soon as the House has ordered the Bill to be printed.

Mr. Baldwin said that last night, in reply to a minute which was sent to the King, the Cabinet received a message from him regretting that he was unable to alter his decision.

This Night Of History

Parliament heard to-night the most momentous pronouncement it has ever heard.

The House of Commons, filled as it has rarely been filled, heard afterwards Mr. Baldwin's sensational speech, reported in full on **Page Three.**

Speeches in the House of Lords, including one by the Archbishop of York, are given on **Page Nine.**

Crowds scenes are described on **Page Four.**

At Fort Belvedere this night the Duke of York is dining with the King.

Mrs. Simpson Told By Phone

Mrs. Simpson was told the news over the telephone at Cannes to-night. It had earlier been announced on her behalf that the King was obviously not visiting Cannes or the Riviera. See Page NINE.

3

A Wartime Princess

On the morning of Friday 10 December 1936 King Edward VIII signed the Instrument of Abdication which, in draft form, had been approved by Parliament the previous day. By the laws of the land, as Edward wrote his name on the final document, he ceased to be king. His brother the Duke of York became the new sovereign, as 'George VI', and Princess Elizabeth became heiress presumptive.

The build-up to the Abdication had been painfully protracted; but the final stages of the drama were contained in just a few days – days of emotion and tension for the nation and particularly for the Royal Family. But if they were days of almost unbearable stress for the King and Wallis Simpson, how much worse were they for the Duke of York, the man who was being left to clear up the mess, to restore the status of a monarchy perhaps damaged irreparably and to shoulder a burden he dreaded.

When George V had been so ill in 1928, the Prince of Wales had made such a lightning dash home from Tanganyika that his brother Bertie joked that it was being said '. . . that the reason of your rushing home is that in the event of anything happening to Papa I am going to bag the throne in your absence!!!!' The exclamation marks are his own, and the idea of Bertie ever *wanting* the throne was as far from the truth in 1936 as it had been eight years before. Unfortunately it was no longer a laughing matter.

In the final stages of the crisis the Yorks had to bear two terrible days in which they heard no news, between 5 December, when Edward formally told Mr Baldwin of his decision to abdicate, and the evening of the 7th when he finally saw his brother to discuss the matter; the King evaded all the Duke's efforts to see him, and for reasons never fully explained, neither the Prime Minister nor any member of the Government communicated with the Duke of York during that time.

To make matters worse, the Duchess could not be at her husband's side to sustain and encourage him, for she was ill with a bad bout of influenza. It was therefore left to the Duke alone to try to explain the situation to his young daughters – an added complication for a father who was as much concerned with Elizabeth's future as with his own. When he went to his mother to discuss what was happening, he broke down, sobbing 'like a child', but except in the strictest privacy, it was the only time he allowed his feelings to overcome him. During the final meetings with his brother, the Duke, closely resembling George V in being unable to express emotion easily, turned his mind to practical matters, devising capital and income for the ex-King when he left the country and a new title for him, 'Duke of Windsor'.

For the Princesses those last dramatic days were exciting and perhaps a little frightening. The reasons for the Abdication were not fully explained, the implications for Elizabeth not stressed in any way. But apart from what they were told by their father and Miss Crawford, the girls could see solemn statesmen to-ing and fro-ing at their home, and they could hear the crowds gathered outside to cheer the prospective king. Their father, grave and preoccupied on his return from the proclamation of his accession, was touched and momentarily taken aback when his young daughters swept him deep curtseys. For Elizabeth it was a strange but wonderful thought that her father and mother were now the King and Queen, but as one whose stated ambition was to grow up to be 'a lady living in the country with lots of horses and dogs', the thought of herself as heiress presumptive did not appeal.

The new Queen Consort set the mood when she told Miss Crawford that, 'We must take what is coming to us and make the best of it.' She enlarged on the philosophy by which she and her husband lived, when she wrote to the Archbishop of Canterbury: 'I can hardly now believe that we have been called to this tremendous task and . . . the curious thing is that we aren't afraid. I feel that God has enabled us to face the situation calmly.'

The new King's first task was to restore the integrity of the monarchy, to revive the Royal Family's image as the focus of complete stability, continuity and respectability it had been in his father's reign. Although, during the distress of the Abdication crisis, he had felt it possible that the whole fabric of the monarchy might 'crumble under the shock and strain of it all', he was helped over the early and most difficult period by the attitude of the people: they felt that their new King had had a 'raw deal', and they were intent on supporting him. Christmas Day 1937 did much to hearten George VI. When he and his family came out of Sandringham Church after the morning service, there was a crowd of six thousand people waiting to cheer them. Gradually, as the weeks went by, his confidence increased, and by dogged persistence and never sparing himself, he learned the job for which he had never been trained. By the end of the first year of the reign, the Archbishop of Canterbury was writing of the people's impression of their King and Queen: 'At first the feeling was one of sympathy and hope. It has now become a feeling of admiration and confidence.'

After all the flurry and excitement of the first days of their father's reign, life for Elizabeth and Margaret settled down to the usual routine, though after 17 February 1937 their home was Buckingham Palace, a vast complex of offices and state rooms as well as living-quarters for the Royal Family, and it took a little while to get used to a home containing six hundred rooms. The schoolroom chosen by the King for

Opposite above *A souvenir postcard to commemorate the coronation of King George VI.*

Opposite below *The Royal Family wave to the crowds from the balcony of Buckingham Palace after the Coronation of King George VI.*

his daughter (the room that had been Elizabeth's nursery as a baby while her parents were in Australia) was bright and sunny, and they found the long corridors excellent for running up and down playing horses, while the huge garden was a delight to the children – and their dogs. The Palace soon became familiar, and when in London, weekends were still spent at Royal Lodge, Windsor, riding, gardening, walking: the simple outdoor pleasures that they all preferred to anything else.

Until the accession, the upbringing and daily routine of Elizabeth and Margaret had been almost identical, despite the four years between them. All through childhood they continued to be dressed in the same style, and even their bedtimes differed only by half an hour. But now Elizabeth was 'heiress presumptive' – that is, heir to the throne unless a brother was born to supercede her rights and become 'heir apparent' (a contingency she is said to have prayed for earnestly every night). It was necessary for her to start learning and doing things that were not the concern of her younger sister. It made no difference to their companionship, but it did sow the seeds of the difficulties Margaret would face when she grew up to find that there was no obvious niche for her to fill.

For the time being, however, the Princesses shared one absorbing, joyous concern: the part they were to play in their parents' Coronation, planned for 12 May 1937.

Queen Mary saw to it that both her grand-daughters thoroughly understood the meaning of each part of the Coronation service, and the symbolism of the orb and sceptres, the ampulla, swords and other coronation regalia. Miss Crawford centred lessons round previous coronations and the lives and qualities of those who had been crowned. And there were fittings for the Princesses of the identical long dresses with long trains, and specially lightweight coronets devised by the King for them to wear at the ceremony.

On Coronation Day Elizabeth and Margaret drove to Westminster Abbey in a carriage with Queen Mary, through streets made unfamiliar by all the stands and decorations, lined with troops to keep back the enormous crowds. The cheering was terrific – some said it was even louder for Queen Mary and the Princesses than for the King and Queen – and once back at the Palace, the family were brought out onto the balcony time and again by the cheers of the gathered crowds that had come to see and applaud them.

Fifteen days after the Coronation, Neville Chamberlain succeeded Baldwin as Prime Minister. He was an efficient Premier in home affairs but a man wedded to a policy of 'peace at any price'. It was a bad time in world history: the Spanish Civil War had began in 1936; in July 1937 Japan began undeclared war on China; by March 1938 Hitler had moved against Austria, and his troops marched in to occupy Vienna. That September Hitler was menacing Czechoslovakia, and although many thought that Britain was committed to stand by her if France did the same, to Chamberlain there seemed nothing shameful in appeasement – it was simply the

Their governess took the Princesses about London to places of interest, often in the company of other children but, as with Pet's Corner at the London Zoo, usually before 'opening time'.

'commonsensical' avoidance of war, regardless of means. His bargaining with Hitler culminated at their meeting at Munich, where the British Prime Minister gave the German dictator all that he demanded. Nevertheless, by the autumn of 1938 Europe was on the very brink of war.

Some see those years between the Coronation in 1937 and the outbreak of war in 1939 as a time of respite, when the pacifist mood of the nation slowly changed to a realization that there was no limit to the demands of the Fascist dictators, and when the country's re-armament programme was at last stepped up.

For the King, still adjusting to the demands of his position, it was a respite too, giving him time to 'grow in stature' and self-confidence, strengthening him for the demands of the war years to come.

For Princess Elizabeth it was generally much the same routine as before, though when she and her sister went on expeditions with Queen Mary, and when Miss Crawford took her charges on some 'adventure' – such as a trip on a London 'tube' train, the attentions of the public were more pressing than before George VI's accession. But Elizabeth's being heir to the throne soon became an accepted part of her life, and increasing public interest was just something that went with it.

They were happy days for the Princesses. Miss Crawford saw to it that they never

Learning to talk to eminent people is a royal requisite.

lacked occupation, and as the King and Queen recognized their daughters' need of wider horizons, a Girl Guide troop for Elizabeth and a Brownie Pack for Margaret were based at the Palace, their members drawn from various walks of life. At a later stage the family pantomimes also involved a partly 'outside' cast – to introduce the Princesses, informally, to a circle of contemporaries, though still the only companions with whom Elizabeth could play on a level of 'equality' were the cousins she met on the yearly Scottish migration to the Strathmores' home. There the King was able to pile hordes of young Bowes-Lyons, Leveson-Gowers and Elphinstones into a car with his daughters and drive off to picnic by the sea – almost like any other family. Otherwise, apart from the time spent with her parents, Elizabeth's days were still passed in the company of Crawfie, Alla, Bobo and Margaret, and the pets that seemed to compensate to a degree for close friends of her own age. By modern standards it was a restricted existence, but Elizabeth never seems to have experienced the frustrations that were to make her own daughter, already enjoying an extent of liberty unimaginable to her mother at a comparable age, want to go to boarding-school.

At thirteen Princess Elizabeth was a dependable child with a fund of down-to-earth commonsense. She had inherited her mother's tranquillity and essentially happy nature, but laced with something of her father's quick temper and a decided will of her own. The Queen is still intrinsically shy, but she learned at a very early age to control her shyness in public and was always quick to remind her sister of the need for politeness and consideration – such as not laughing if she noticed someone

A first meeting between Elizabeth and Philip – at Dartmouth Naval College in 1939, when she was a little girl in a beret, and he was a dashing young cadet.

in a funny hat. Elizabeth could be as gay as the extrovert Margaret, but she was by nature more serious-minded. She was born receptive rather than creative. Margaret was soon displaying an enviable ability to play the piano by ear. The Queen still quite often displays her talent for mimicry when she is talking about someone, but when they were children it was the irrepressible Margaret, exhibiting her brilliant aptitude for the same gift, who could reduce her father to helpless laughter even when he was annoyed with her. Nevertheless, if, despite himself, the King spoiled his impish younger daughter, there was a special bond between him and Elizabeth, and she seemed to have a precocious understanding and appreciation of the devotion to public service and great sense of duty that ruled his life.

In the summer of 1939 the Royal Family cruised along the south coast of Britain in the royal yacht *Victoria and Albert*. The King's aide on this occasion was his cousin and former shipmate Lord Louis Mountbatten, Elizabeth's 'Uncle Dickie' (later Earl Mountbatten of Burma). It was through him that the Princess came to know his nephew Prince Philip of Greece, when the royal yacht brought them to Dartmouth Naval College where Philip was studying.

In fact, the Prince and Princess were distant cousins, as both were descended from Queen Victoria, but before 1939 they had met on only a couple of occasions, once when Elizabeth was eight, at the Duke of Kent's wedding, and again at George VI's coronation.

Although Philip was a Prince of Greece, he had seen very little of his homeland. His father, Prince Andrew, a brother of King Constantine I of Greece, was banished from his country during one of its periodic revolutions, and Philip shared his parents' exile in France. He grew up an energetic, tough little boy, his natural independence strengthened by an education that included an English preparatory school, a term or two at Salem, Kurt Hahn's famous school in Bavaria, and some years at Gordonstoun, also founded by Hahn, where the emphasis was – and still is – on initiative and self-reliance. And the visits he had paid to illustrious relatives spread round Europe had turned the gauche schoolboy into a young man of considerable charm.

By the summer of 1939, Philip had been a cadet at Dartmouth for only a few months, intent on making a career in the Royal Navy. When the royal party arrived at the College, they found most of the boys quarantined with chicken-pox, and in case of infection the Princesses were confined to the Captain's house, with Philip detailed to entertain them.

The sentimental favour the Dartmouth encounter as the moment when Prince Philip first turned his thoughts to love and marriage, but it seems very unlikely that, at eighteen, he was ready for anything more than light flirtation. Elizabeth, at thirteen, was far too young and ingenuous for that. But she and her sister had had few boy-companions, and Philip was very attractive.

Leaving Dartmouth, the *Victoria and Albert* cruised northwards, finally depositing the Royal Family to continue their trip overland to Balmoral. On Sunday

Queen Elizabeth with the Princesses Elizabeth and Margaret in the garden at Windsor Castle.

3 September, when the air-raid sirens started wailing in London as Neville Chamberlain finished delivering the declaration of war, the Princesses were still in Scotland. The King spent that holiday in Scotland more than usually involved with what turned out to be the last of the boy's camps, started when he was Duke of York. And the Queen and their daughters joined him round the traditional huge bonfire that always ended camp, where the leaping flames spiked the darkness where Balmoral pipers marched and played. The family joined the boys in singing favourite songs, and as the last notes of 'Auld Lang Syne' died away, their domestic peace began sliding away too.

It had been an unusually sunny summer, the oppressive heat adding to the sense of uncertainty and foreboding, yet the holiday-makers, gas-masks tucked into their picnic-baskets, crowded the holiday resorts and remained apparently carefree. For

Nowadays the Queen has little time for gardening, but as children she and Margaret enjoyed giving a hand with the hoeing in their rambling garden at Royal Lodge, Windsor.

all the slit-trenches being dug in city parks, the sand-bags and anti-aircraft-gun emplacements, the searchlight sites and national preparations for war, the idea of real hostilities seemed so remote to the majority that they clung optimistically to the hope that all would yet be well.

The announcement on 22 August 1939 of the Soviet-German Pact of Non-Aggression stunned the Allies and sent the King and Queen hurrying to London. Elizabeth and Margaret remained behind in the charge of Miss Crawford.

There was a British expeditionary force in France, but both Britain and France were avoiding any major operations against the enemy, and the war entered the strange, unreal first phase of what the French called *'une drôle de guerre'*, the Americans, more realistically, 'the phoney war'. The anticipated bombing did not occur immediately: tragedies at sea were the only reminders that Britain was actually at war. People became a little careless with the blackout; gas masks were not so evident; children evacuated to the countryside began filtering back into the cities.

The Princesses remained in Scotland until Christmas on what was officially termed an extended holiday. In fact, Miss Crawford had been asked to continue the usual routine of lessons and amusements, and Elizabeth's specialized tuition in constitutional history from the Under-Provost of Eton College, begun in the spring of that year, was continued as a postal course. A French teacher was also imported one or two days a week to supplement the curriculum.

As usual every spare minute was spent in the open air regardless of the weather. And those first months of the war produced an unrecognized bonus for Elizabeth and Margaret: with the diminution of the royal household for the war-effort, there was no one to act as groom for their ponies, and so with much enjoyment and satisfaction the Princesses took over the job themselves. During that time in Scotland Jock and Hans were kept out at grass, so the work was not very onerous, but the girls' new duties did involve outwitting a wily pony set on not being caught, grooming, saddling and bridling, as well as the various forms of 'training' which the riders thought up for themselves. Their comparative isolation also meant that, within reason, and as long as they kept in sight of the policeman toiling along the track behind them on a bicycle, for the first time in their lives Elizabeth and Margaret could ride where and when they liked, learning to cope on their own with all the little incidents that befall children and ponies everywhere. There is a photograph of Elizabeth's sturdy, bronze-coloured pony, which the Queen has since inscribed: 'Jock – who taught me more than any other horse'.

Up in Scotland, as the heather faded on the hill, as peaty pools became rimmed with ice and the chill wind brought the first flurries of snow, the war seemed very remote, but the King realized that nowhere was immune to parachute attack, and in the New Year he brought the Princesses back to Royal Lodge, Windsor, where they remained until the end of May.

On 4 April 1940 Prime Minister Neville Chamberlain announced that he thought Hitler had 'missed the bus' by not attacking during the previous winter, but by 9 April German troops had invaded Denmark and conquered that country and Norway by the end of the month. The great parliamentary debate of 8 May, that forced Chamberlain to resign and brought Winston Churchill to the premiership, preceded the start of the German *blitzkrieg* ('lightning war') by two days. German tanks and air power ensured the fall of the Netherlands, Belgium and France by mid-June.

After Dunkirk, when flotillas of gallant little boats somehow contrived to bring the bulk of the British Expeditionary Force home to fight another day, the Princesses went to live in the greater security of Windsor Castle. There, guarded by a battery of anti-aircraft guns and troops to repel air-borne invaders, with the cellars bomb-proofed, air-raid shelters in the courtyard, and the crown jewels stacked away in the vaults, Princess Elizabeth spent the remaining years of the war and of her own childhood. Despite its proximity to London, Windsor seemed as safe as anywhere, and the family could be together whenever the King and Queen could be persuaded to leave the capital for a few hours.

They were dark and terrible days when Churchill was promising the country little but 'blood, toil, tears and sweat' yet at the same time – and contrary to reason – inspiring complete confidence in eventual victory. Today the Queen is proud to know that her parents would not contemplate sending her and Margaret to the safety of Canada. She saw for herself the lattice-work of vapour-trails criss-crossing the sky as 'the few' took on the myriad invaders during the Battle of Britain. When the bombing was stepped up, she saw, night after night, the flames distorting the outline of London, only twenty-three miles distant, heard the crashing reverberations of gun-fire, felt the age-old walls of the Castle shake to the explosions of the 'block-buster' bombs. There were nights when she and Margaret and Alla had to hustle down to the shelter in their night clothes, and moments of excitement and sometimes of fear to interrupt the daily routine. Like many of her age the war

The King and Queen with Prime Minister Winston Churchill, surveying the damage to Buckingham Palace. The King and Queen endured the four-year blitz alongside millions of Londoners, and went out to cheer and sympathise with their people after the night raids.

Above *A treasured moment of
family life together during the war.
The Royal Family at Buckingham
Palace in 1942.*

Left *Although the Queen is four
years older than Princess Margaret,
as children they were always
dressed alike. A formal portrait
by Marcus Adams, 1941.*

deprived Elizabeth of social life and contacts and she grew up in very sheltered circumstances. But if her youthful activities were curtailed by the war, her knowledge of current affairs most certainly was not. Important affairs of state would not be discussed with a child but she was there in the centre of it all and could not avoid being caught up to a degree in national events.

The Queen remembers with pride how her father (that diffident, sensitive man, so loath to become king, so reluctant to contemplate the thought of war) would only consider his Prime Minister's plans for his safety, in the event of invasion in 1940, if he could then become head of a resistence movement. All through the war years he travelled indefatigably up and down the country, visiting and encouraging fighter-pilots, bomber-crews, naval units, defence corps and assault troops; in the later stages of the war George VI flew thousands of miles to inspect and inspire his forces overseas. The King and Queen went around London and the provincial towns and cities after the bombing raids, to see and talk to the people in each devastated area. And by the end of those weary years the King, the focus of the spirit of the times, had won such universal esteem for his sense of service and courage that he had forged a bond with his people such as the monarchy had never known before.

In October 1940, at the suggestion of the BBC, Princess Elizabeth made a short broadcast, addressed principally to the children of the Empire, assuring them that '. . . we children at home are full of cheerfulness and courage. . . .' Coached by her mother, the Princess sounded clear and at ease, but it must have been something of an ordeal for a fourteen-year-old.

As for most young people of her age, there was not much in the way of normal entertainment or socializing for Princess Elizabeth, growing up during the war years. As the years passed, one or two small informal dances were held for her, and the Christmas pantomimes were encouraged – partly to help her overcome her shyness, but otherwise most of the Princess's leisure was spent in reading and sketching, riding and driving the ponies, and walking the dogs. All too rarely could Prince Philip, by then an officer in the Royal Navy, manage a short leave and 'blow in' to spend it, by standing invitation, at Windsor Castle.

Philip had passed out of Dartmouth in 1940 – after winning the prize as best cadet, and the King's Dirk as the best all-round cadet of his term, and much to his frustration he had been posted as midshipman in the battleship *Ramillies*, on escort duty in the safe area of the Indian Ocean. It was an appointment reputedly devised to keep this prince of a neutral country out of any potentially embarrassing situations, such as being wounded, captured, or worse still, killed in action. But the Italian invasion of Greece in October 1940 destroyed Philip's technical neutrality, and he was soon on the operational scene, where he saw plenty of action. He was in the naval bombardment of Bardia, on the Libyan coast, only three days after joining *HMS Valiant*, and was in the thick of the lively operations off Sicily that followed soon after. Philip was nineteen when he was mentioned in dispatches and

Left *Elizabeth and Margaret consulting the script with their director, in preparation for a performance of 'Aladdin' at Windsor Castle in December 1943.*

Right *The Princess eventually managed to persuade the King to allow her to do war service. As a Second Subaltern in the Auxiliary Territorial Service she learned to maintain vehicles at the Aldershot depot in Hampshire.*

decorated by Greece for 'efficiency in carrying out orders' during the rout of the Italian fleet off Cape Matapan in March 1941. He was twenty years old, and Elizabeth fifteen, when, in England working for his sub-lieutenant's examination, he started taking up invitations to visit the Royal Family. As an ex-serving naval officer himself, the King enjoyed Philip's usually light-hearted accounts of wartime life in the senior service, and he and the Queen welcomed the young man's lively company for their daughters. Philip teased both sisters indiscriminately, shared jokes with Elizabeth and no doubt partnered her if he happened to be at the Castle for one of those informal dances. Philip was at Windsor for one or two Christmases and in 1942 joined the audience of the pantomime *Aladdin*, in which Elizabeth soared to unusual heights of animation in her role of principal boy.

When Philip went back to sea, he and the Princess started writing to each other – but there was no story-book romance about the correspondence. Seen in retrospect, Prince Philip thinks it *might* have been highly significant if he had not been a relative: he sees those Windsor visits and the ensuing correspondence as no more than the Royal Family's natural order of friendliness, extended to a young relative with no particular home ties of his own.

Possibly that is also how the Royal Family viewed it. There may have been a hint in the family of a possible marriage in the future, but, according to Prince Philip,

only on the lines of, 'he is eligible, he's the sort of person she might marry . . .', but the King would dismiss anything of that sort as belonging to a time so far in the future that it need not even be contemplated. As for Elizabeth herself, few if any would have known what she was really thinking about Philip. After all, her obvious devotion *could* have been the continuing hero-worship of a child.

In 1941, the German offensive into Russia secured the Soviet Union as an ally for Britain, together with the USA when Japan attacked Pearl Harbour. Despite the renewed retaliatory bombing of British cities and towns, 1942 saw the beginning of the end for the Germans in Russia, and naval victories in the Pacific that stemmed the further advance of the Japanese in south-east Asia and Burma. In October British victory at the battle of El Alamein marked the turn of the tide: the Germans and Italians were ejected from North Africa by May 1943, and the Allies' invasion of Sicily and Italy forced the Italians to make a separate peace in the autumn of that year.

In April 1944, when Princess Elizabeth was celebrating her eighteenth birthday by attending (in her capacity of honorary Colonel-in-Chief) a special 'birthday parade' of her own regiment, the Grenadier Guards, Prince Philip was a first lieutenant in *HMS Wallace*, in the Pacific.

The King, determined that, unlike himself, his daughter should be thoroughly

71

grounded in the duties she would one day inherit, was stepping up Elizabeth's opportunities for insight into affairs of state. Officially she would not be eligible for the duties of a Counsellor of State for another three years, but Parliament had already amended the Regency Act to allow her a seat on the Council. When the King flew to visit his forces in Italy that summer, Princess Elizabeth, with members of the older generation of the Royal Family, was appointed to act as a Counsellor, with the Queen as always heading the list.

In the meantime the war in Europe had entered its last, savage phase. All over Britain the final preparations for 'D Day' (the plan called 'Operation Overlord' for the invasion of the Continent) were progressing steadily. On 6 June the four-thousand-strong invasion fleet landed in France. By 16 June, the first tense days safely accomplished, the King was at last able to fulfil his ambition to go to the Normandy beaches and inspect conditions for himself. And on his return that night, Elizabeth, with her mother and sister, was able to hear a first-hand account of the most crucial combined services operation ever attempted.

On the previous night a wave of Hitler's first secret weapon, the flying bombs, had come clanking in over the Channel to bring further death and destruction to Britain, depressing public morale, by the 'inhumanness' of their pilotless flight, more than the worst of the conventional bombing. Six hundred 'doodlebugs' exploded in London alone during the first fortnight, killing nearly two thousand people, wounding thousands more and damaging over two hundred thousand homes. At Buckingham Palace so many windows were smashed so many times that panes made of plastic material replaced the glass.

Some months before the final capitulation of Germany, Princess Elizabeth, by then nineteen, realized one of her dearest ambitions. Although, with all others of her age, she had had to register for war-work after her sixteenth birthday, her father had always refused her pleas for 'real work'. Now, however, the King at last agreed to her joining one of the women's services, and she became a subaltern in the Auxiliary Territorial Service. She was driven daily to Camberley, to learn, among other things, vehicle maintenance and how to drive a lorry. (And maybe that course accounts for the fact that, in the privacy of her own grounds, the Queen handles a car with above-average expertise and demonstrates the same liking for speed as other members of her family.)

On 8 May 1945 the end of the war in Europe brought Londoners in their thousands to the Palace, to cheer the coming of peace and applaud their King and Queen who had been through it all with them. Princess Elizabeth was not with her parents on all their appearances on the Palace balcony: at the instigation of the King, and with some young army officers to look after them, she and her sister were in the crowds, savouring the exhilaration of the mass emotion of thankfulness and joy.

Opposite VE Day Celebrations. Top *A thronging crowd outside the Palace.* Centre left *Exuberant US airforcemen atop a London doubledecker bus.* Centre right *Princess Elizabeth and Princess Margaret in the crowds with a WVS worker.* Bottom *Greeting the victorious people — Mr Churchill, the King and Queen and the Princesses.*

4

A Princess at Home and Abroad

Early in 1944 Prince Philip asked his cousin the King of Greece to approach George VI on his behalf about the possibility of his future marriage to Elizabeth. The British King was adamant: he and the Queen liked Philip; they were proud of the young man's war record; they approved of his outlook and ideals; they did not rule out the possibility of his marriage to Elizabeth in a far-distant future, but there could be no question of a formal courtship at that time. The Princess was not quite eighteen, and if her father could no longer ignore her very apparent feelings where Philip was concerned, the Prince was still the first and only young man she knew well, and there was always the chance that she might come to prefer another. Maybe the king did not appreciate to what his 'Lilibet' had inherited his own persistent character.

After her eighteenth birthday Elizabeth began to emerge into public life, usually appearing with the King and Queen but also undertaking an increasing number of engagements on her own – launching ships, taking the salute at marches-past, attending public functions. It was all part of the duties of an heir to the throne. But the Princess had another reason for wishing to play her part as fully as possible: she wanted to help her father. The King was tired, physically and mentally drained by the stresses and strains of the war years that followed so quickly on the heels of his accession; and the coming of peace had brought new problems – the war-debt, economic upheavals, industrial re-organization, food shortages – worries which beset the King as much as his ministers. So the Princess set out to alleviate the burden on him by taking on as many public duties as possible.

Nevertheless, Elizabeth still found time to enjoy a full social life. London society would never return to what it had been before the war, and Princess Elizabeth could never know the social freedom that her daughter was to enjoy, but the King and Queen encouraged her to accept 'suitable' invitations, held small dances for her at the Palace and asked young people – in particular young Guards officers of suitably noble birth – to spend weekends at Windsor and Sandringham. But however many eligible young men had the honour of dancing with or squiring Princess Elizabeth, the name increasingly included in her conversation was 'Philip'. It was the only name that ever mattered, there were other friends but no other boyfriends, and when the Queen is talking to anyone today his name crops up just as frequently. Queen Mary

Opposite Elizabeth and Philip pictured with Princess Margaret after their engagement on 10 July 1947.

understood her grand-daughter very well when she added steadfastness and knowing her own mind to Elizabeth's virtues.

For most of the summer of 1945 Prince Philip was still on active service, but when he was on leave, the Press noticed the many social functions at which he and the Princess were both present – though they were being very discreet. By the spring of 1946 the King (still looking on Elizabeth as a child - though she was now twenty years old) was having to take stock of the situation. He would not have been the first father to dread losing an adored daughter, to fear the disturbance of a home life that was the centre of his happiness, but in this case there were other considerations: a royal marriage, and more particularly the marriage of the heir to the throne, has to be considered at a national level.

The foremost problem was Philip's nationality. He is not, of course, a true Greek: the kings of the Hellenes, his paternal ancestors, were of Danish origin, with no native Greek blood; his mother, Alice of Battenberg, was a grand daughter of Queen Victoria, and her parents had always made their home in Britain; but an added complication was the fact that his four sisters had married German princes – and after the recent war, that was no asset to Prince Philip. He had been trying for some time to obtain naturalization as a British subject, so that his commission in the Royal Navy could become a permanent one, but owing to the shifting and complex state of Greek politics, it had still not been confirmed: he was, in fact, high in the line of succession to the Greek throne.

Despite the unresolved problems, when Prince Philip, on leave in the late summer of 1946, went to stay at Balmoral, he and Elizabeth settled the matter between themselves. They became engaged. Faced with the accomplished fact, the King acquiesced but for the time being insisted that it must be a secret engagement, known only to the immediate family. In the months that followed, the Prince was away from London, doing an instructor's job at Corsham, though his MG sports-car frequently headed for Buckingham Palace, entering unobtrusively through the tradesmen's entrance. The couple's first real parting was not until early 1947, with the long-planned royal tour of South Africa.

The Royal Family sailed on 1 February, leaving behind the worst winter within living memory. They landed at Cape Town on 17 February to an exuberant welcome and the start of a strenuous programme entailing their travelling many thousands of miles by aeroplane, train and car. On their return to Cape Town Princess Elizabeth celebrated her twenty-first birthday, the first coming–of-age of an heir to the throne ever to occur in a Dominion. The day was declared a public holiday; the Princess reviewed the South African Army, and, before the brilliant ball given in her honour at Government House, she made a broadcast. It was a simple, sincere message to all her father's people, a pledge of duty that she has been faithfully carrying out ever since: '. . . I declare before you all that my whole life, whether it be long or short, shall be devoted to your service. . . .'

During the tour there was one item of news relayed to the Royal Family, an announcement carried in the *London Gazette* of 18 March 1947, that made Princess Elizabeth very happy and solved one problem: Philip was now a British subject and wished to be known simply as 'Lieutenant Philip Mountbatten RN – taking the surname by which his mother's brothers had been known since their renunciation of German titles some years earlier. The King was prepared to grant him the title 'His Royal Highness', but the honour was declined at the time, a gesture that impressed the King and was typical of the Prince.

If the King had hoped that his daughter might use the separation from Philip to reconsider her commitment to him – or at least to postpone the marriage which George VI feared would 'break up' his happy family, he was to be disappointed. By the time the Royal Family returned from South Africa, no doubts were possible – though even then there was a further two-month delay before the engagement was officially announced.

Then, on 10 July 1947, the Court Circular announced the royal engagement: the King and Queen 'gladly gave their consent' to the betrothal of their daughter the Princess Elizabeth to Lieutenant Philip Mountbatten RN – and everyone then knew what many had been suspecting for some time. On the evening before, during a family dinner party that included Princess Alice, Philip's mother, at the conclusion of a short speech by the King, Prince Philip had slipped a ring onto Elizabeth's finger. He wanted it to be a special symbol in his own family and so it

Princesses Elizabeth and Margaret in South Africa. It was during the tour of South Africa with her parents in 1947 that Elizabeth made an impressive twenty-first birthday broadcast pledging herself to be of service to the nation.

was made up, to a design chosen by his fiancée, of diamonds from a ring given to Philip's mother by his father many years before.

By the end of July the King had formally approved the marriage at a meeting of the Privy Council. Soon those few sections of the public who had been rumbling about the Princess making an 'alien' marriage, joined those who were enthusing over Philip's blond, Viking good looks, recalling that his mother was a grand-daughter of Queen Victoria, that Edward VII's consort, Queen Alexandra, had been of the Danish royal House, and that the very popular Duchess of Kent was Philip's cousin Marina, a Greek princess.

With no more need for tactful secrecy, Elizabeth and Philip could show the world the happy faces of a young couple in love. They were fêted and applauded wherever they went. Wedding presents poured in from rich and poor, from Britain and the Dominions – with a food-parcel or two from the United States where some were convinced that the British were starving, along with hundreds of pairs of nylon stockings, an almost unobtainable luxury in post-war years. Almost all were put on show at St James's Palace, with admission fees to go to charities.

The weeks began to fly. Philip, who had been baptized into the Greek Orthodox Church, had his position regularized by admission into the Church of England. There was the problem of compiling a list of wedding-guests, with numbers dictated by the size of Westminster Abbey. What proved to be rather inadequate arrangements for coverage of the wedding ceremony were made for the British and Dominion Press. The King at first vetoed filming in the Abbey but was persuaded to change his mind. Official interest, to do with the import-regulations, in the silk used for the bridal gown, was satisfied when it proved to be of Chinese origin but British weave. All these details, and many others, were part-and-parcel of the business of preparing a royal wedding.

George VI now awarded Elizabeth and Philip the Most Noble Order of the Garter, the oldest order of English chivalry, and Philip was authorized by the King's personal prerogative to take the prefix 'His Royal Highness' (although he did not officially become a British royal prince until 1957). On the day before the wedding, the King created his future son-in-law 'Duke of Edinburgh, Earl of Merioneth and Baron Greenwich', but as the titles were not announced until the next morning, up to the marriage ceremony he remained Lieutenant Philip Mountbatten RN.

Since the days of Queen Victoria, who had gone to her Coronation and to the celebrations of her Golden and Diamond Jubilees in brilliant sunshine, the term 'Queen's weather' had come to mean a fine, sunny day. Queen Elizabeth II is not so lucky, and nowadays 'Queen's weather' is all too often rainy. But on her wedding day, 20 November 1947, the rain held off, and the fact that the day was grey and cold made no difference to the enormous number of people who had every intention of being out on the streets to cheer the royal bride. And there was plenty of brilliance and colour in the procession from Buckingham Palace to the Abbey to dispel, if only for a day, the continuing austerity that was the order of the times.

A fairytale princess on her wedding day – Elizabeth photographed by Baron, renowned for his royal photography.

The troops lining the route were still in wartime khaki, but King George had agreed to let austerity go by the board as far as the Household Brigade was concerned. Out from the moth-balled security of the past eight years came splendid full-dress uniforms, and the crowds were treated to the almost-forgotten sight of black bearskins and burnished chin-straps, the red-striped trousers and blue tunics of the Foot Guards, the red-plumed helmets of the Royal Horse Guards, the nodding white plumes of the Life Guards, trotting by on black horses as gleaming as their riders' drawn swords, breastplates and polished boots. The elegant horse-drawn carriages that headed the cortège – Queen Victoria's Irish State Coach, the 1902 State Landau, Queen Alexandra's State Coach, the coaches and barouches normally kept in the Royal Mews – had all survived the war, as had the red and gold semi-state livery of the coachmen and footmen. There came Queen Elizabeth with the seventeen-year-old Princess Margaret, the chief bridesmaid, their carriage drawn by a pair of the famous Windsor Greys. There was Queen Mary, dignified and gracious, straight as a ram-rod. Next came a selection of the more important foreign royalty who had flocked from the Continent to attend the wedding.

As the cheering rose in a crescendo, there at last was the Glass Coach – usually given pride of place because the specially wide windows give the best possible view of the occupants, so the throngs who had made their way to London from every quarter of the British Isles, and many from the Dominions and other countries overseas, had at least a glimpse of the people they had come to see. There was the King, wearing the uniform of Admiral of the Fleet, looking proud and happy, and there was Princess Elizabeth beside him, her wedding-dress of white satin scattered with garlands of white York roses, worked in pearls and entwined with ears of corn embroidered in crystal. There were pearls at her throat; a diamond tiara held the veil in place over her brown hair.

Inside the magnificent nine-hundred-year-old Abbey, the Princess Elizabeth Alexandra Mary and Prince Philip were married in the sight of a huge congregation of royalty and statesmen, peers, peeresses, bishops, knights and the various denominations of the less exalted. The Archbishop of Canterbury performed the ancient rites, using the same simple form of service as that employed at any Anglican church wedding in the land. After the service they walked down the long nave hand in hand and out into the greetings and rapturous cheering of half a million people. Back at Buckingham Palace the excited crowds had the bridal pair out on the balcony with the King and Queen three times before they could join their 150 guests, waiting in the white and gold supper room to enjoy a wedding breakfast. The table was decorated with sprigs of heather and myrtle, from a bush struck from a sprig in Queen Victoria's bouquet. Pipers supplied the music, Philip and Elizabeth cut the cake with the sword once belonging to his great-grandfather, Louis of Battenberg. And at about four o'clock the Duke and Princess Elizabeth Duchess of Edinburgh left by carriage to catch a train, with a favourite corgi and two hot-water bottles snuggled under the rug, the bride sporting a fetching blue felt beret adorned with ostrich feather pompons – that became an immediate best-seller in the United States at the equivalent of 13s a copy.

The honeymoon was to consist of two parts. Firstly they went to Broadlands, Lord Louis Mountbatten's beautiful home near Romsey in Hampshire, that Philip knew so well from schoolboy days. Then, after a day or so the Duke of Edinburgh and his bride drove north, to the greater seclusion of Birkhall, near Balmoral, for Elizabeth the scene of so many happy childhood memories.

Broadlands, Lord Mountbatten's beautiful home at Romsey, Hampshire, which has recently been opened to the public. Prince Philip stayed there frequently in his youth, and he and Princess Elizabeth were loaned the house for the first part of their honeymoon – from here they went north to Balmoral.

They returned to London in time to celebrate the King's birthday on 14 December and as a temporary measure settled in apartments in Buckingham Palace. Living with 'the in-laws' is not an ideal situation for any young married couple, even in a house of those dimensions, but they had little option: Clarence House, which was to be their first London home, was being renovated and was not ready for occupation until 1949, and Sunningdale Park, near Ascot, given them by the King as a proposed country refuge, had burned down before they could move in. Early in 1948 Windlesham Moor, a manor house in Berkshire, was 'rented' for use at weekends. Under the circumstances, ordering the meals was more or less the limit of Princess Elizabeth's housewifely duties in those early days, but when they were off duty, she and Philip had the interest of overseeing the alterations to Clarence House.

For the first six months of their marriage Prince Philip had an unexciting but conveniently placed job in the Operations Division at the Admiralty, but in addition to taking joint engagements with the Princess, and supporting her when the occasion was one for her alone, Philip was also starting out on his own account on the royal path – chairing committees, making speeches, a smooth 'running-in' that was to lead eventually to the unprecedented working partnership, individualistic yet totally co-operative, that the royal couple have now been enjoying for so many years.

When the Admiralty job came to an end, Prince Philip began a staff course at the Royal Naval College, Greenwich, which necessitated his 'living in' during the week, but he could still get occasional time off for royal duties.

For a man used from boyhood to making his own way in life, it cannot have been easy for him to learn to accept second place on those first public occasions. But 'to sustain' had been Philip's original pledge, and Elizabeth was soon finding the most onerous functions lightened and made easy by a delightful and reliable companion, whose 'asides' produced humour out of situations where protocol had never before dared a smile. And occasionally, as when her husband took his seat in the House of Lords and when he received the freedom of London and the same honour at Greenwich, it was she who sat and watched and did the sustaining.

In May 1948 Elizabeth and Philip had a gentle introduction to royal tours overseas. They made a very successful official visit to France, where the welcome was almost overwhelming, and the crowds of people and photographers a

An official visit to France was the first overseas commitment for Princess Elizabeth and Prince Philip. It was a great success, despite some criticism by strict Sabbatarians for dining in a restaurant on Sunday.

reminder to Philip that the privacy of his former days was a thing of the past. It was hurtful to arrive home and read criticism in the Press, by strict Sabbatarians, of their two innocuous Sunday relaxations – a visit to the races at Longchamps in the afternoon, and later dinner in a fashionable restaurant overlooking the Seine. But that was another reminder of something all members of the Royal Family come to accept, that it is virtually impossible to please everyone all the time.

In the autumn of 1948 the pattern of Elizabeth and Philip's life as young newly-weds changed to that of young parents: their son, Charles Philip Arthur George,

Proud parents! Princess Elizabeth and Prince Philip with Prince Charles, aged nineteen weeks. This photograph, taken at Buckingham Palace, was the first showing the new family together.

was born at Buckingham Palace on 14 November. The baby was greeted with joy in the Royal Family as the first male in direct line of succession born for sixty years. Blue fountains played in Trafalgar Square to mark the occasion. His parents, like most, considered their baby son the most wonderful ever, but this baby was more than that. He was heir to the throne that his mother would one day inherit, and on his upbringing and the outlook of his parents rested much of the success he would one day make of life, as a man, and as a king.

But a cloud hung over the Royal Family's happiness: King George VI was ill. The previous spring the King seemed to have recovered at last from the strains of the war, but he soon began to develop bouts of cramp and pain in his feet that

Charles and his young mother had a lot of fun together. These photographic portraits of Princess Elizabeth and her son, by Cecil Beaton, are considerably less formal than those taken of Elizabeth when she was a toddler.

became continuous. It was characteristic of the king that he did not tell his daughter of his pain until after her baby was born – the doctors' first alarming report of October had been kept to himself. The King continued with even his most exacting commitments until the arrival of his grandson, despite the specialists' confirmation of the diagnosis, hardening of the arteries, with a threat of gangrene and possible amputation of one leg. A public announcement was made only on 16 November. Among other treatment, he was prescribed rest, and though by the New Year 1949 he was able to undertake a few public duties, King George reluctantly agreed to postpone the Australia and New Zealand tour planned for the following spring. But an operation soon became imperative, and though the King made a good recovery from it, he had to slow the tempo of his life.

It was a very busy time for Elizabeth, and for Philip, who found additional leave was necessary for extra commitments. They were at last able to move into Clarence House that July, and the business of setting up house had to be fitted into their heavy schedule of public engagements. The year 1949 was not the easiest time to establish a new home: 'austerity' was still the key word in post-war Britain; but Clarence House was furnished almost entirely with wedding-presents. Elizabeth, always practical, thoroughly enjoyed discussing such items as the siting of electrical points with her husband, an enthusiast for modernization.

By October the King was so much better that Philip was able to resume an active naval career and flew to Malta to join *HMS Chequers* as first lieutenant. The Princess joined him in November, staying until after Christmas, when the ship was detailed for patrol in the Red Sea, and again for a short while in April 1950. On each occasion there was some criticism of her leaving her small son Charles – in the care of two devoted nannies and his adoring grandparents! Her visits to her husband

In Malta there were a few public engagements, but mostly it was a delightful taste of service life, with picnics and polo and impromptu parties for entertainment.

A christening portrait of Princess Anne who was born on 15 August 1950, the day that her father was gazetted Lieutenant Commander, and given his own ship, HMS 'Magpie'.

included a few semi-ceremonial duties for the Princess, but otherwise her life at the Villa Guardamangia, on the outskirts of Valetta, (loaned them by Earl Mountbatten), was as carefree as that of the other young officers' wives. It was an unprecedented pleasure for the Princess to go out shopping and to the hairdresser, to sit chatting on the sidelines of the polo field with other players' wives. She and Philip threw impromptu parties at the villa; there were picnics in the countryside, by the sea, and in boats. When *Chequers* sailed for Alexandria in April, Elizabeth returned home to await the birth of her second child.

There is only fifteen months difference in age between Prince Charles and his sister. Princess Anne Elizabeth Alice Louise was born on 15 August 1950 – a double celebration for her father, recently gazetted lieutenant-commander with his own first command, the frigate *Magpie*.

And so, while Elizabeth was happily occupied with Charles and the new baby, once again Philip had a job after his own heart, turning *Magpie* into 'cock ship' of the squadron and keeping her there. Then, in November that year, he flew to Gibraltar to represent the King at the opening of the Legislative Assembly. Later in the month Elizabeth again flew out to join him.

This time the couple undertook a semi-official visit to Greece, and as *Magpie* did not possess accommodation suitable for the commander's wife, the Princess sailed in convoy in the dispatch vessel *Surprise*. It was a delightful voyage across the Ionian Sea and through the Gulf of Corinth and the Corinth Canal, with the kind of sunrise that only Greece can produce and a typically sudden storm in which Elizabeth disproved the myth that she is a bad sailor. Athens was *en fête* for their arrival, but there was good opportunity between the ceremonies for Philip to show his wife his homeland, if not the island of Corfu where he was born.

Home again, the Princess continued successfully to combine her public duties with being an excellent mother to two lively children, and the efficient running of her household. In both roles her relaxed, down-to-earth outlook, combined with her sense of fun, stood her in excellent stead. There is no-one better than the Queen at good-humouredly chivvying a reluctant small boy bent on procrastinating up to bed, and as parents she and Prince Philip have two big assets. They have adapted their traditional methods of bringing up children to modern times, and have always been in complete agreement about decisions concerning their family. By May Philip was home on special leave for the ceremonial opening of the Festival of Britain. Two months later he came home for good.

The Queen and Prince Philip in the Grand Entrance, Buckingham Palace.

5

Accession to the Throne

The Festival of Britain in 1951 was designed to mark the country's recovery from the war. It was good advertising to the world at large, a good boost to public morale. Press photographs showing the King standing on the steps of St Paul's Cathedral to open the Festival on 3 May, caused much public concern at his tired, drawn appearance.

Three weeks later he was ill with what appeared to be influenza. His recovery was worryingly slow, and by the time Prince Philip arrived home in July (on the indefinite leave that in fact was to mark the end of his active service with the Navy), his presence was urgently required. Queen Elizabeth, Princess Margaret, the Duke and Duchess of Gloucester, the Princess Royal, the widowed Duchess of Kent, even the indomitable eighty-four-year-old Queen Mary, were all taking their share of the royal duties, but because of their position the lion's share had to fall to Princess Elizabeth and her husband. In addition to home engagements, in the autumn they were to represent the King on a tour of Canada and a visit to the United States.

All through the remainder of that summer the Royal Family's anxiety increased. The King was not making progress, and on 8 September an X-ray confirmed his doctors' worst suspicions: George VI had cancer of the lung, and an immediate operation was necessary. It was a critical operation, made even more dangerous by the likelihood of a thrombosis, but although his life hung on a thread, the King survived; gradually some of his strength returned, and by the middle of October he was writing to tell Queen Mary that at last he was feeling a little better.

At one stage it was felt that the heir to the throne could not leave the country, but in fact the Canadian tour was postponed only a week or so, although a part of the original plan had to be abandoned. Princess Elizabeth and Prince Philip were to have crossed the Atlantic in the ship *Empress of Britain*, but when at last their plans were agreed, there was then no time to go by sea. Although other members of the Royal Family had been crossing the Atlantic by plane for years, there was an archaic embargo on the heir to the throne doing so. To Prince Philip this appeared an excellent opportunity to overcome the opposition, and since it was a case of either flying or cancelling the entire project, his voice prevailed, and they flew by Stratocruiser to Montreal.

On 8 October 1951 Princess Elizabeth set foot on Canadian soil for the first time. She and her husband were greeted by Prime Minister St Laurent and Field Marshal

The Canadian tour was undertaken on the ailing King's behalf in the autumn of 1951. It entailed travelling thousands of miles by car, train and aeroplane, yet it was an immense success and gave the young royal couple their first taste of a full-scale overseas visit together.

America's President Truman was so touched by Princess Elizabeth's youth and sweetness that he wrote to King George VI: '. . . As one father to another we can be very proud of our daughters . . .'

Elizabeth pictured in protective waterproof clothing during her visit to Niagara Falls.

Viscount Alexander, then Governor-General, and they began the first of those much appreciated but very exacting overseas programmes that were soon to become an accepted and essential part of their duties.

At the beginning of the tour Elizabeth had been tired and tense after the anxieties of the past weeks and, shy by nature, appeared withdrawn and unsure of herself. She was still desperately anxious about her father, and it did not make for a happy situation to know that she had with her a sealed envelope containing the draft of her accession declaration in case of his sudden death. But Philip was there to relieve the pressures, backing her up with his natural charm, a little tetchy when he thought she was being overtaxed, unbuttoning protocol with his own brand of amusing

Sir Walter Raleigh laid his cloak for Elizabeth I to step on, but this cowboy used an Indian blanket for Princess Elizabeth when she arrived at the Calgary Exhibition grounds for the famous stampede.

'mock up' press photograph to include both Princess Elizabeth
d Prince Philip when square-dancing at Government House in
ttawa. The Queen loves to dance, and after the intricate Scottish
els at which she is adept, she found square-dancing to a 'caller'
th easy and great fun.

informality and providing the supporting role he has undertaken on these many such programmes ever since. With her husband's help, Elizabeth was very soon relaxed and enjoying herself.

On the thirty-five-day coast-to-coast tour, inevitably extended beyond the originally less arduous conception, there were balls and banquets, civic receptions, military inspections, presentations, speeches, an enjoyable private square-dancing party, visits to Niagara Falls and the equally famous Calgary Stampede, and innumerable 'whistle-stops'.

The couple thoroughly enjoyed their three-day visit to the USA, as guests of the President, though the Princess found American security precautions a little disturbing (to Prince Philip they seemed irritatingly absurd). But the visit was a great success. And President Truman was so touched by the contrast between Elizabeth's youth and sweetness and her shy, formal greeting that he threw protocol to the winds and replied with a paternal, 'Thank you, my dear . . .'.

The entire tour was a triumph, and the Canadians, some of whom had been slightly cautious beforehand, were completely captivated by the royal couple. On their return, George VI demonstrated his pride and delight by making Elizabeth and Philip Privy Counsellors. They found the King looking frail but cheerful and obviously feeling much better. He was looking forward to going to South Africa with the Queen, in the coming March of 1952, to recuperate in the warm sunshine. His family stifled the dread that perhaps he might not live to get there, and allowed themselves a little hope.

That Christmas at Sandringham there was no room for sad thoughts. The King was so happy there, surrounded by those he loved best, confident of an eventual return to good health, that his optimism was infectious, and even the doctors seemed satisfied with their patient's progress.

Since their return from Canada on 17 November, there had been little leisure for Elizabeth and Philip. On the 19th they had driven in state to the Guildhall to attend a civic luncheon given by the Lord Mayor to welcome them home. Their engagement-calendar for December included a midnight matinée in aid of Prince Philip's special interest, the National Playing Fields Association; they accepted honorary degrees at London University; and the Princess also received the Cymmrodirion Medal from the organization of London Welshmen, celebrating the society's two-hundredth anniversary at St James's Palace. Public functions tailed off for the Christmas holiday, but on 31 January 1952, they flew from London Airport in the BOAC aircraft *Atalanta* to Kenya, the first leg of another important and extensive overseas mission in the King's name, to East Africa, Australia and New Zealand.

The previous evening the King had taken a family party to see the popular musical *South Pacific* at Drury Lane, his first visit to a theatre since his illness. The next day he was at the airport with the Queen and Princess Margaret, to inspect *Atalanta* and have a last-minute chat with Elizabeth and Philip, and then to wave them farewell, standing bareheaded on the tarmac.

It was goodbye.

Sometime during the early hours of 6 February 1952, after a happy day's rough shooting at Sandringham, while he was peacefully sleeping the heart of King George VI stopped beating.

The exact hour of the King's death is not known, but at the time when she unknowingly became queen, Elizabeth was at 'Treetops', a hut built in a giant fig-tree in the Abadare Forest game-reserve, from which visitors could watch a salt-lick and drinking-pool where big game were illuminated in artificial moonlight. The past few days had been filled with functions and ceremonial, set against a

Winston Churchill said: '. . . his life hanging by a thread from day to day — and he, all the time cheerful and undaunted . . .' The King waved a last farewell to Elizabeth and Philip at London Airport as they left for Kenya on 31 January 1952.

After the sudden death of her father Elizabeth returned home as Queen Elizabeth II. The recognizable figure of Prime Minister Churchill, accompanied by Clement Attlee and Anthony Eden, waits at the foot of the steps to pay homage to the new queen.

kaleidoscope of brilliant colour and movement and clamour from the ebullient crowds, and carried out under the scorching heat of the African sun. There was an afternoon's safari in Nairobi National Park where Elizabeth, in those days the photographer in the family, was able to get good shots of zebras and giraffes and a handsome lion gorging itself on its kill. Then they had spent two peaceful days at Sagana Lodge, the small house set in the foothills of Mount Kenya on the edge of the Nyeri Forest, that had been a wedding-present from the people of Kenya.

The original Treetops cabin, since burned down, was not very far away, and Elizabeth and Philip went there to spend most of the night on the balcony, watching entranced as elephants materialized silently from the gloom of the trees, rhinos lumbered into sight to quench their thirst, and a couple of waterbuck fought for supremacy, battling in and out of the shadows.

Early the next morning the Princess and her husband returned to Sagana Lodge. The tragic news from England did not reach them until after lunch. The message was given to Philip, and he told Elizabeth.

Since she was a little girl the Princess had been trained in royal behaviour, how to subdue emotion in public, how to rise to the demands of her position. In the privacy of her own rooms she could be the young daughter grieving for the father she loved; in the eyes of the world, even in those of her own staff and officials, she was the Queen.

For Philip, lately forced by circumstances out of his chosen career, now face to face with the changes in their life he had been praying some miracle would avert for a while longer, it was a shattering moment of truth. But his thought had principally to be for Elizabeth, and fortunately for both of them there was much to do. They were out of Sagana Lodge within the hour.

On the evening of the next day, 7 February 1952, Her Majesty Queen Elizabeth II, a small, courageous figure, walked down the steps of the aircraft just landed at London Airport, to be greeted by her Prime Minister, Winston Churchill. She was driven to Clarence House, where the royal standard fluttered in the dusk, telephoned her mother at Sandringham and received Queen Mary – 'her old Grannie and subject', driven over from Marlborough House, to be 'the first to kiss her hand'.

The next day the first of her duties was to make the accession declaration to her Privy Counsellors at St James's Palace. The Queen told them she prayed that 'God will help me to discharge worthily this task which has been laid upon me so early in life'. 'My heart is too full', she said, 'for me to say more to you today than that I shall always work as my father did.' From St James's Palace and three other points in London, from a number of other British towns and cities and aboard Her Majesty's ships, the new sovereign was proclaimed.

Like his father's before him, for a few days the body of George VI was lying in Sandringham Church watched over by his gamekeepers. When the King's coffin was lying in state in Westminster Hall, draped with the royal standard, the diamond-studded Imperial Crown, the sceptre and orb, and the wreath from his widow lying on top of the bier, a quarter of a million of his people came to do homage. And for a few minutes, scarcely noticed in the shadows, three Queens stood together, mother, wife and daughter, there to mourn and watch, while the crowd silently filed past.

Again, they gave a sailor king a sailor's funeral, with naval ratings to haul the gun-carriage carrying the coffin to its resting-place in the vault below St George's Chapel, Windsor. Next in the cortège came the carriage with the Queen, the Queen Mother, Princess Margaret and the Princess Royal, and walking behind it the Duke of Edinburgh, the Duke of Gloucester, the Duke of Windsor and the young Duke of Kent.

Queen Mary was not there. From her window in Marlborough House she watched the cortège taking her son's body from Westminster Hall to Paddington Station. She did not feel strong enough to do more. In her long life she had mourned four monarchs and three sons, the fourteen-year-old Prince John, an epileptic who died in 1919, the charming Prince George, a war casualty, and now 'Bertie', the King. It was enough, and now her own time was not far off.

Queen Mary, the epitome of all she felt that royalty should stand for, died on 24 March 1953, only three months before her grand-daughter was crowned. It was sad that Mary, who had always had such justifiably high hopes of the new sovereign, did not live to see her coronation.

There had been little time for Elizabeth to adjust to all the great changes and responsibilities of her new life, or for the nation to recover from the death of a beloved King and adjust to the romantic expectations of the new reign. But as the decorations went up in London and celebrations were planned in every town and village, excitement grew to fever pitch.

It rained on the night before the Coronation, and on into the early morning of Coronation Day itself, 2 June 1953, damping the slumbering forms of the thirty-thousand people camping out along the processional route; the rain ran in rivulets down the tents of those units of the armed forces under canvas in Hyde Park, Kensington Gardens and other London parks; military wet-weather orders were issued concerning 'Colours' (flags) to be 'cased until they reach the assembly areas'. It drizzled on and off all through the Coronation Day, but not even a monsoon could have dampened the spirit of those who proudly took part in that vast procession, or of the thousands more gathered to watch the splendid cavalcade marching, officially at 112 paces a minute, past the decorative flags and banners, beneath the glittering arches (lion and unicorn rampant above, symbolic crowns suspended below). Perhaps the late Queen Salote of Tonga, 'the tallest sovereign of the smallest kingdom', personified the general feeling that day as she drove in an open carriage through the rain, on the return from the Abbey, so obviously delighted, if very wet, and smiling and waving with infectious exuberance to the appreciative crowds.

The Coronation of a sovereign as young and popular as Queen Elizabeth II generated immense excitement and anticipation throughout the land. Industrious and elaborate preparations were made.

Below *A special commemorative crown issued by The Royal Mint.*

Above *Flags and bunting were prepared.*

Left *Coronation stamps issued by The Post Office.*

Left *China mementoes designed by J. Wedgwood & Sons.*

Below *A birds-eye view of the Coronation procession to Westminster Abbey.*

Above *The Coronation in Westminster Abbey of Elizabeth the Second by the Grace of God of the United Kingdom of Great Britain and Northern Ireland and of Her other realms and territories Queen, Head of the Commonwealth.*

Left *Coronation mementoes: an egg-cup, a spoon, a mug, and a clock surmounted by a picture of the Queen riding the Metropolitan police-horse Winston to the Trooping the Colour.*

Opposite left *The approved souvenir programme issued for the Coronation.*

Opposite right *A glass claret-cup issued to commemorate the Coronation.*

Opposite below *After the Coronation the Queen appeared on the balcony of the Palace to watch the RAF fly past. She was accompanied by her Maids of Honour and the Royal Family.*

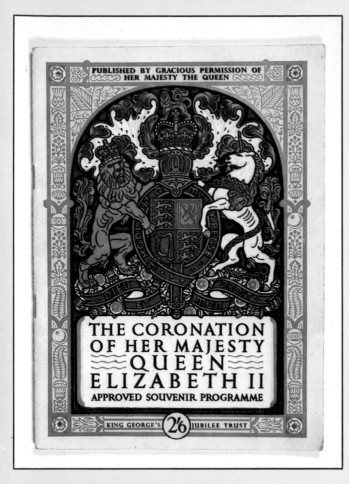

The Lord Mayor of London's procession was the first abroad that morning, leaving the Mansion House just before eight o'clock, with that of the Speaker setting off from the House of Commons one and a half hours later. Both were riding in their own coaches. A little earlier the motor-car procession of 'Certain Members of The Royal Family' left Buckingham Palace, with another of royal and other representatives of foreign states, seventy-two countries in all, leaving St James's Palace at much the same time. At 9.15 a.m. the carriage procession of Colonial Rulers left the Palace, followed at short intervals by that of Colonial Prime Ministers, and another special carriage procession of princes and princesses 'of the Royal Blood'. The Queen Mother and Princess Margaret, riding in the Glass Coach and accompanied by a State Landau conveying their suite, set off from Clarence House at ten o'clock.

At 10.26 a.m. precisely, preceded by a mounted officer of the War Office staff, four troopers of the Household Cavalry, five companies of Foot Guards, the band and corps of the Welsh and Irish Guards, another five companies of Foot Guards, and the King's Troop, Royal Horse Artillery, The Queen, with the Duke of Edinburgh beside her, set out on the route that led to her crowning in Westminster Abbey. Her conveyance was the Gold State Coach, constructed for George III as 'the most superb and expensive of any built in this kingdom', velvet-upholstered, with panels decorated by Cipriani, gilded, ornate, twenty-four feet long, weighing four tons, and used for every coronation since that of George IV. It was drawn, strictly at the walk, by eight Windsor Greys, the four nearside horses ridden and controlled by bewigged postilions, and accompanied by fifteen footmen, the Yeoman of the Guard, four divisions of the Sovereign's Escort, the Queen's Bargemaster and twelve Watermen. The coach was flanked by high-ranking officers and dignitaries, all mounted, the Master of the Horse, the Lord High Constable, Gold-stick-in-Waiting, Silver-Stick-in-Waiting, with personal aides-de-camp and equerries to the Queen riding immediately behind.

Following on for mile after mile and augmented on the longer return route, some on horseback, some conveyed in yet more carriages and cars, the majority marching on their feet, came Admirals and Field Marshals and Air Commodores, and brass and silver and bagpipe bands, contingents of all three Services of the United Kingdom, officials and personnel of the Civil Defence and Civil Services, with detachments from the defence forces of every Commonwealth country and colony.

It was a splendid spectacle, a fitting tribute to the rightful pomp and majesty by historical tradition surrounding the throne and one which through the media of television was seen all over the world. But for the Queen the essence of that day, the moment for which she had been preparing herself, came in Westminster Abbey: Queen Elizabeth came to her crowning with full awareness of and awe for its religious meaning, dedicating herself to all the weighty responsibilities symbolized in the ancient rituals.

Opposite *A formal study by Baron, 1953.*

The Queen Mother with Charles and Anne on the terrace of Royal Lodge, Windsor – her country home after her daughter's coronation.

Elizabeth II was crowned amid the clichéd but very real 'blaze of loyalty'. Quite apart from the natural warm enthusiasm and excitement emanating from the crowds on Coronation Day, which was to be expected at the beginning of such a young and popular sovereign's reign, there had been an underlying, unprecedented and exceptional wave of emotionalism centring on the Queen and increasing in intensity as Coronation Day approached. This was born largely of the anti-climax and privations of the post-war years, becoming a fixation on the Queen as the inspiration of a 'new Elizabethan era' of prosperity and progress.

The late King had longed for more time to give his heir further coaching in her future job, but he had already grounded her well. Queen Elizabeth surprised her Ministers with her good sense and judgment, her grasp of detail and ability to make the right decision quickly. Winston Churchill, mourning the King and friend he knew so well, had seen his new sovereign as 'a mere child', but after only one or two of the Tuesday evening audiences customarily given by the Queen to her Prime Minister, Churchill speedily became one of his monarch's most devoted admirers. And there was general approbation for the way in which Elizabeth performed her new ceremonial duties. Court mourning curtailed the extent of her public functions, but the Queen held her first investiture on 27 February, 1952, only three weeks after her accession; she went to Westminster Abbey on the Thursday before Easter, to carry out the ancient custom of distributing specially minted silver coins, 'Maundy money', to the 'deserving', their number matching that of the Queen's age. There was another investiture on 2 April, and on the 21st of that month, the Queen's twenty-sixth birthday, she made a last inspection of the Grenadier Guards as their Colonel, having become, as Sovereign, their Colonel-in-Chief.

There were a number of 'first times': the first time the royal cipher 'ER' had ever been seen in the sky, executed by planes from the RAF Central Flying School at Little Rissington; the Queen's State Opening of Parliament, the first of her reign; and, on 5 June, her official birthday, she made history at the Trooping the Colour as the first queen regnant for four hundred years to ride at the head of her military cavalcade. But that ceremony was not new to the Queen. At the age of twenty-one, mounted side-saddle (a form of equitation learned specially for the occasion), wearing a special dark-blue uniform and mounted on a quiet ex-hunter specially schooled for the job, she had accompanied the King at the parade, riding in the traditional position of the heir to the throne. The next year the King had not been well enough to ride, and his daughter, wearing the becoming adapted uniform of one of the five regiments of Foot Guards, had ridden beside his carriage. After that she had deputized for the King until his death. Since her accession the Queen (mounted originally on a Metropolitan police horse and more recently on Burmese, presented by the Royal Canadian Mounted Police) has taken the salute every year at this spectacular military ceremony.

Private life under the new circumstances required a good deal of adjustment. The family did not leave Clarence House immediately after the accession; only after that Easter holiday, as usual spent at Windsor, did they move into the Palace – described by Prince Philip, only half-humorously, as 'a museum' and their own 'tied cottage'. It was a wrench to leave the home they had made together and go back 'behind bars', as the Queen, less seriously, put it. At one point there was even an idea of their remaining at Clarence House and using the Palace purely as the working centre that essentially it is. But the scheme was dropped. Like King George VI, they moved back 'over the shop', and the Queen Mother and Princess Margaret made their home at Clarence House.

If the Queen found the extent of her new duties arduous and difficult, it was the nature and scope of his that perplexed her husband. When they married, Philip had accepted that part of Elizabeth's life could never be his, and in their early years together they had resolved the problem and made a start on what has proved such a very successful working partnership. Now, when Elizabeth became queen, there were many others to take over where before there had been only Philip. Now, understandably, some of those whose proud life-work it was to serve the Crown felt, and showed, little need for the aid of the man who is the Queen's husband but not the king, a consort in marriage but not officially the Prince Consort, and who is certainly not capable of becoming a cipher.

As usual, Philip's concern was not principally on his own account. He could echo Winston Churchill's words: 'I fear they may ask her to do too much.' He had no wish for a part in the inner mysteries of the monarch's work; he had already refused the Government's suggestion that he should look at state papers – a decision that left him without responsibility to any government department and so, bounded only by common sense, free to voice his own opinions and make his own suggestions. But he was convinced of his own ability to make a worthwhile contribution towards easing his wife's burden – and it was a question of sorting out, without offending others and with a patience that does not come easily to one of his temperament, how best to set about it.

It took time for the Queen and the Prince to evolve that 'division of labour' which is an essential ingredient of the happy, helpful companionship they have achieved through the years. It took time, too, for Philip to carve out the career he created for himself, without any foundations to build on.

In 1952, among other engagements, he visited an aerodrome, became the first member of the Royal Family to fly at 500 m.p.h., descended a coal mine in a 'hoppit' bucket, and enjoyed himself at the Road Research Laboratory at Harmsworth. These were pointers to the sort of interests he might pursue. As the newly installed Chancellor of the University of Wales, the Prince's maiden speech to the undergraduates was also a foretaste of the future: it contained real knowledge of his subject, a spicing of ready wit and a core of plain sense. Nearly thirty years later, the same ingredients are still there in the eighty to ninety speeches the Duke of Edinburgh makes annually, speeches that are stimulating and challenging – even if their occasional abrasiveness does sometimes cause trepidation in high places.

The front cover of 'Picture Post' in September 1954 shows the Queen on her way to the Lord Mayor's luncheon, held to welcome her back from her Commonwealth tour.

18 September, 1954

PICTURE POST

THE QUEEN'S
SUMMER
Four-page Colour Souvenir

4d

18 SEPTEMBER 1954

THE DAY AND NIGHT FIGHT FOR THE HARVEST
WILFRED PICKLES IN GERMANY—Exclusive Pictures
BRITAIN'S TOP-OF-THE-BILL GIRL CROONERS

HULTON'S
NATIONAL
WEEKLY

VOL 64 • NO 12

6

Royal Leisure

When the Royal Family moved to Buckingham Palace, Charles was nearly four-and-a-half and Anne was almost two-and-a-half. They had the same nurseries on the second floor that the Queen and Princess Margaret had had as children, and which Margaret had been using as her private apartments since the end of the war.

Up to the move from Clarence House, nursery life had remained typically conventional and much the same as it was when the Queen was a child. Then quite soon afterwards Mabel Anderson, engaged originally as under-nurse, took over. Under her affectionate, no-nonsense care, the same standard of good manners, obedience and thought for others was insisted on, but there was a cheerful, easy air about it all that relaxed any nursery formality. It was symptomatic of the freer outlook that in photographs of the family 'off duty', Charles and Anne wore not the 'best suits' and frilly dresses of previous years but the jeans and jerseys of 'ordinary' children.

The biggest differences between the Queen's upbringing and that of her children began when Charles was eight. From the age of five he had been doing lessons in the Palace schoolroom with his governess, the late Miss Peebles, but he then went to a pre-preparatory school for a few hours each day. Going to school was contrary to all precedents for the education of the heir to the throne, but the Queen and Prince Philip knew that home education was no basis for a 'normal' upbringing. They were looking towards the future, and a public education and learning to mix with people were essentials for a modern king in a modern world.

Charles started his unenthusiastic and rather timid entry into school life in a furore of unwanted attention from Press and public that nearly wrecked the whole idea, by making it impossible for him to start at the beginning of term; combined with tonsilitis and then the removal of his tonsils, these difficulties reduced the time that he could spend at Hill House. But it was sufficient to give him a gentle breaking-in for the next big step forward, his admittance as a boarder at Cheam, his father's old preparatory school.

Charles was a sensitive, very shy little boy, very dependent on the adults who surrounded him – and from infancy he had been used to living with many adults (Palace staff and visitors, as well as his family). For years he remained considerably more at ease with grown-ups than with his contemporaries. Like many sons,

Opposite The Queen enjoys a happy moment with some of her labradors at Balmoral. Photograph by Patrick Lichfield.

"-LOOK WHAT I GOT FROM A BOY AT SCHOOL--!"

A cartoon of 1955 by Emwood. Prince Charles had just started at Cheam, his first school.

Charles adds a specially close relationship with his mother to the love that children have for both their parents. It cannot have made it any easier for the Queen, suffering the usual qualms of a mother sending her small boy to boarding-school for the first time, to know that Charles was very homesick and never really enjoyed his time at Cheam. But she and Prince Philip do not make important decisions lightly, or then fail to carry them out, whatever their personal inclinations: they saw it as essential for Charles to face up to his new life, so that he would later be able to stand up to whatever life threw at him; when he was old enough, he adopted the same philosophy for himself.

With Anne it was not entirely the same. The Queen has never been quite certain that the comparative freedom of school did not make it harder for her daughter to adjust to the restrictions of her adult life. But by the age of twelve Anne was feeling that she had outgrown a governess, educationally and otherwise; she wanted other company and outside interests. So in September 1963 she began life as a boarder at Benenden School for Girls in Kent.

The chief reason why Anne enjoyed her schooldays was that she was quickly absorbed as 'one of the crowd'. But the ordeal of arriving as a new girl was not made any easier by finding her 320 potential school-mates, all the staff and a sprinkling of Press men assembled outside the entrance to greet the Queen – and, perforce, herself. Anne has always been more athletic than intellectual, but although her 'A' level examination grades were not as good as the school had hoped, she obtained two passes, and six at 'O' level, at the first attempt. She inherited the family inability to cope with mathematics and was inclined to work hard only at the subjects that interested her. The Queen was always able to point out to her husband that the comment 'could do better if she tried harder' on some of her daughter's reports, was an echo of the remarks which had sometimes appeared on his own!

Through the years the Queen has become accustomed to the way people tend to become suddenly self-conscious in the presence of royalty, but it was particularly sad when it affected her as a parent, when Prince Andrew was at preparatory school. She used to enjoy going to the usual parental occasions, but when she realized that everyone immediately became 'different', she felt it was bad for her out-going, happy-go-lucky second son and curtailed her visits.

As adults Charles and Anne thoroughly enjoy each other's company and share the same rather zany brand of humour and a love of speed and life in the open air. Otherwise they are very different in temperament and tastes. For Charles classical music and opera are ingredients of living; Anne has always had a preference for 'pop'. He enjoys the live theatre; she likes films. Flying is one of Charles's greatest joys; Anne used to say that any form of transport other than a horse or a car driven by herself made her feel travel-sick. Nowadays Charles plays polo, Anne 'events', though they both participate in the hazardous sport of competitive team-riding across-country. When they were young, Anne was the more talented and keener

Prince Charles and Princess Anne share a mutual liking for speed.

rider and the Prince, perhaps tired of being admonished to 'Use your *legs*, Charles!' by a younger sister, gave up riding until he began to play polo when he was about fifteen.

As children, Charles, amenable, unsure of himself but with a built-in awareness of what was required of him, and Anne, adventurous, bossy and apparently self-sufficient, argued frequently and not always amiably. But those occasions, like Anne's short-lived but tempestuous tantrums, were reserved for the nursery. Both the Queen and Prince Philip had the enviable knack of quelling their children when young with little more than a look or word. They made no material difference between the two elder children in the earlier days, but in retrospect Prince Philip thinks that perhaps his daughter did resent being a girl, second in the family to a brother who, as heir to his mother's throne, was 'more important' than herself.

As Charles and Anne grew older, they were encouraged, but not coerced, to do the kind of things that might stand them in good stead in the future. Once the children were of an age to make sensible decisions, their parents followed the commendable practice of giving them the pros and cons of anything concerning themselves and then, within reason, leaving them to make up their own minds.

There was public argument about whether it was a good or bad idea to send Charles to Gordonstoun, his father's old school, but it was beside the point: Charles was given the alternatives and himself chose to go there. His decision was soon

Left *The Queen and Prince Philip find the parental role one of the most rewarding. Strolling in the gardens at Frogmore, Windsor.*

Right *Prince Andrew found that there was usually something interesting to watch from the nursery windows at Buckingham Palace.*

justified by his success at Gordonstoun: with his retiring nature, the rough and tumble of public school life was more harassing for him than for one of Prince Philip's ebullient temperament, but, like his father, he rounded off his career there as Guardian (Head) of the school, a position conceded entirely on merit. Then, after his degree course at Cambridge and Aberystwyth Universities, it was his own choice to take a short commission in the Royal Air Force and follow that with a five-year stint in the Royal Navy.

Like most parents – although with more publicity – the Queen and Prince Philip received plenty of gratuitous and unsolicited advice on how to bring up their children, but the public were more quiescent over the younger two than they had been about Charles and Anne, or perhaps more trusting, and maybe Andrew and Edward have also benefited from their parents' more relaxed attitude to them. As young boys they were a friendly, natural pair and refreshingly direct.

The Queen and Prince Philip believe that, as children grow up, the parental place is in the background, to be there only when wanted. Once their elder children had left school, they encouraged them to lead their own lives, apart from public engagements. Charles, on vacation from University, took full advantage of his liberty, and if it was not quite as simple for Anne, she had her own circle of friends and spent as much time as she could with her horses. But still, when the family was together at the Palace, Anne and Charles never failed to go and chat with their

Right *Breakfast under the eye of a television camera during the making of the 'Royal Family' film in 1968. This unprecedented film about the Queen and her family was produced by a BBC/ITV consortium and has been seen by more people throughout the world than any other documentary film. (All of the pictures that appear on these pages are stills from 'Royal Family'.)*

parents after breakfast – otherwise the Queen and Prince Philip did not see very much of either of them, and were content that it should be like that.

Weekends at Windsor and holidays in Scotland and Norfolk were and remain a different matter. The Royal Family enjoy a very close and happy relationship, appreciating the only company in which they can really relax. Royal annual holidays in Scotland have been something of a ritual since the days of Queen Victoria, with traditional picnics and walks and typical Scottish sports, such as salmon-fishing and deer-stalking.

Far left Princess Margaret with her children David, Viscount Linley born in 1961, and Lady Sarah Armstrong-Jones who is three years younger.

Above left Prince Edward was sometimes more interested in the television cameras than in the film making.

Above Prince Philip enjoys strenuous sports but also gains much satisfaction from his above-average talent for painting.

Right The Duke and Duchess of Kent and their two elder children, George and Helen.

A couple of Range-Rovers, or one car and a kind of miniature bus, drawn up outside the front entrance of Balmoral Castle have replaced the entourage of horse-drawn carriages that stood there in Queen Victoria's day. But when the cars set off, loaded with family and guests, picnic-baskets and dogs, the Queen, at the wheel of the leading vehicle, chooses a track through the heather on the hill which like her destination, would have been familiar to her great-great-grandmother. The picnic site may be the favourite one beside Loch Muick, where there is a solitary little house, looking out at the water and flanked on two sides by tall scotch firs, which

Left *Riding on the 'hill' at Balmoral — the perfect relaxation in a public life of protocol. The Queen with a young horse, Benbow.*

Above *Prince Philip includes fishing amongst his less active pastimes.*

Above right *A royal home where jets do not thunder overhead and the public are not admitted. The Queen and Prince Philip and their younger sons enjoying the peace and freedom of Balmoral.*

Right *Prince Philip administers the royal estates and he and the Queen like to discuss farming policy 'on the spot' whenever they can.*

was built for Queen Victoria, on a spit of annexed land for which King George VI eventually had to pay. And because the Queen has affection and admiration for that other illustrious queen regnant, she renews the interior to keep it exactly the same as on the day when her great-great-grandmother last closed the door behind her.

Inside Balmoral Castle the décor still includes much of the tartan designed by Victoria's Prince Consort, Albert, and the custom Victoria inaugurated, of a kilted piper marching up and down outside the Castle and her other homes to greet the day, is still continued. Otherwise, there is little about the over-all informality

and the unrestricted companionship between the age groups of Royal Family life today that Queen Victoria would either recognize or approve.

The chief function of the family's private life is to provide them with relaxation and relief from the formality of their public existence. That is one reason why picnics are so popular, with Prince Philip taking over the barbeque while the Queen demonstrates that she is a dab hand at making salads; there is something for everyone to do – and never any staff to do it for them. When shooting is the order of the day, in the butts for grouse in Scotland, on a pheasant-drive at Sandringham, the

Queen brings out the picnic lunch and joins her family and guests, driving herself, her gun-dogs in the back of the car.

For years the Queen has been breeding a now famous strain of labradors at Sandringham. She enjoys giving the youngsters a little training and working them herself on the estate. When she can spare the time, she watches with the keenest interest the prowess of her own dogs at field-trials. The Queen still takes the same pleasure in her animal companions that she did in childhood. When she is 'off duty', in London or anywhere else, her corgis are always around, and out in the grounds of her country homes at least some of the labradors are there at her heels. She will stop and call to dogs in the kennels and laugh at the baying response to her voice. A call from the window of her car as she drives past one of the fields brings her horses cantering over to see her.

Sandringham and Balmoral are the Queen's private property, and Prince Philip took over the administration of the estates soon after the accession, as one load he felt he could well carry for the Queen: he has succeeded in making the farms at Windsor and Sandringham viable enterprises. Country life is the Queen and Prince Philip's chief mutual interest in their leisure; during the few weeks after Christmas which the family spend at Sandringham, the Queen often plods out in mackintosh and gum-boots to make plans on the spot with Philip, about crops and cattle and improvements to the gardens; she and her husband enjoy dropping in at the various farms and cottages to renew their friendships with their tenants. Those weeks at the

The Royal family enjoy one another's company while walking on the estate at Balmoral.

'big house' give them the chance of meeting their country neighbours and taking some part in the life of the countryside.

It takes a lot to keep the Royal Family indoors when they are on holiday. On the coldest January day they will take off for Holkham, not far from Sandringham, for a session of beach-combing, followed by uproarious and necessarily energetic games (such as chasing an old tyre not quite in reach of the thunderous waves). In the evening Sandringham, cosy and 'homey' for all its size, calls for huge log fires, good to sit by when watching favourite television programmes, reputedly documentaries or something on the lines of *Dad's Army* or *Kojak*. But the family are not television addicts, and when there are household gatherings, most of their entertainment is homemade, and distinctly more hilarious than erudite. It nearly always includes sessions of that extrovert, inhibition-shedding version of charades disarmingly called 'The Game', much enjoyed by the Queen – but cordially loathed by her former Prime Minister the late Sir Winston Churchill.

Sometimes the Queen is able to find a few days in the spring to go back to Sandringham, so that she can see the latest crop of foals bred at the stud. The Queen has a wonderful 'eye' for a horse and she has become one of the few acknowledged world experts on the intricate subject of thoroughbred blood-lines. Since she always works out the mating programmes for her own mares, in due time she has the excitement of following the racing fortunes of some of the animals resulting from her own decisions. Usually there are about twenty to twenty-five royal horses

Except for formal occasions, where the Queen goes her dogs go too.

The Queen has a great rapport with her horses and likes to visit and talk to them even if she is not riding. The stable-yard at Balmoral.

in training, but it is a bonus year when the Queen can find time to attend race-meetings other than the Derby and Royal Ascot Week. During the flat-racing season she keeps in constant communication by telephone with her racing-manager and trainers, discussing progress, racing-schedules and results.

Racing is a hobby that the Queen shares only with her mother – the rest of the family have a strong preference for participation rather than the more static role of spectator. The Queen likes to ride whenever she can: and once a year she appears on horseback on a racetrack. That is for the strictly private and much enjoyed scamper up 'the straight' during Ascot Week instituted by the Queen years ago, an excursion which incorporates many of the family and guests from the royal houseparty and which nowadays is usually won by Princess Anne.

The riding-horses are housed in the Royal Mews at Windsor, and some accompany the family on holiday. As their work is not very arduous, the Queen has been able to enjoy the company of her three or four favourites for many years. There is the black mare Burmese which she rides at the Trooping the Colour, Bellboy, bred at Sandringham and a half-brother to the well-known Columbus, and Cossack, once described by Princess Anne as being 'very Russian!', sired by a little Karabach stallion presented to Prince Charles many years ago by Russian Premier Kruschev.

These are the horses that provide the Queen with the happy relaxation she needs. At weekends, during holidays and whenever she has the time, the Queen chooses one of these good companions to ride in the Park at Windsor, or for galloping across

Opposite *The Queen and the Queen Mother with the Duke of Beaufort at the Badminton Three-Day Horse Trials – an annual and much enjoyed outing for the Royal Family, where the crowds respect their privacy.*

Above *Like her husband the Queen is a keen photographer, and the various activities of her family provide plenty of scope.*

the flat, open Norfolk fields, or wending her way through the heather on the hill at Balmoral.

Thoroughbreds are not the limit of the Queen's horse-breeding activities. Her interests extend to the Highland and Fell ponies used as deer- and working-ponies at Balmoral, and also to the Haflingers bred there since a pair of these sturdy mountain ponies were presented to her during a state visit to Austria in 1969. In the days before Prince Philip gave up polo, the Queen used to try to breed him suitable ponies from the ex-polo mares at Sandringham, but unfortunately her efforts were not very successful: Prince Philip seldom got on with the home-bred animals. But she now has the satisfaction of knowing that three bred at Sandringham are included in Prince Charles' polo string.

The same stud has produced three horses that have made their name for her in a very different type of sport. The first was Doublet, bred by the Queen as a potential polo-pony for her husband. When the chestnut grew too big – Prince Philip teases his wife about over-feeding her young horses – he was sent to Alison Oliver, Princess Anne's trainer, as a possible event-horse for her. At the time, both rider and horse were inexperienced, and the chestnut was not the easiest of characters, but with hard work and determination on the part of all three of them, the Princess and Doublet formed a rewarding partnership. In 1971, when they took on top eventers from eight different countries, including six former Olympic riders, the Queen and Prince Philip were there to watch with pride and delight as their daughter, riding a home-bred horse, became Individual Three-day Event Champion of Europe for that year.

During the Doublet era the Princess had a couple of young horses in her string, both belonging to the Queen, bred at Sandringham and sired by Colonist, a notable ex-racehorse that once belonged to Sir Winston Churchill. The magnificent grey Columbus was eventually ridden to victory at Badminton in 1973 by Captain Mark Phillips, who now competes with him in hunter trials and cross-country team-riding. Indeed, it was through a mutual interest in eventing that Princess Anne met the man who was to become her husband. The other horse, Collingwood, was sold but returned to the fold in 1979 to become a successful mount across-country for Prince Charles. When the talented and much loved Doublet broke a leg at exercise, the Queen's Goodwill replaced him and was the horse her daughter rode in the 1976 Olympics.

Fortunately the Queen has a very philosophical attitude towards the hazards connected with her family's sports. In the days when both Prince Philip and Prince Charles were liable to the falls and occasional damage inevitable for those who play polo (a game the Queen would have loved to play herself), she was already of the opinion that a spot of danger adds spice to most sports. She was genuinely amazed when someone suggested that Charles should not have played polo just prior to his investiture as Prince of Wales.

In the years since, the Queen has had many reasons for retaining this rational frame of mind. When a damaged wrist and his fiftieth birthday decided Prince Philip to forego polo, he took up driving a 'four-in hand' – a coach drawn by four horses, which he handles himself. The competition includes a course across-country taken at a sufficient speed to remain within a tight time limit. The Prince has had no more spills than other exponents of the art – though his are more publicized – but coping with an overturned carriage, perhaps minus a wheel and still attached to four frightened horses, is not everyone's idea of a peaceful occupation. However, the Queen has always understood the necessity of violent exercise for a man of her husband's temperament and in his position.

Like his father, Prince Charles is a qualified jet-plane and helicopter pilot and enjoys flying himself. He genuinely enjoys jumping out of aeroplanes with a parachute, and his appetite for 'doing things' once led him to perform a simulated escape from a stranded submarine, a feat so hazardous (despite its taking place in a tank with stand-by life-savers) that the Queen and the Prime Minister had first to give their permission. Fortunately Prince Philip taught all his children to swim in the pool at Buckingham Palace, as it is a help to Charles that he took to the water like a

When Prince Philip gave up polo he took up competitive driving. Practising with a pair on the Long Walk, Windsor Castle.

fish, when it comes to surfing in the Australian breakers, scuba-diving and the relatively new sport of wind surfing. His strong swimming, plus a special rubberized suit, enabled him to try the risky pleasure of walking under the Arctic ice. The Queen knows that her eldest son is liable to embark on some sort of adventure wherever he may be, and she understands his reasons for doing so.

Anyone who rides in horse-trials accepts the fact that falls are an inevitable part of the sport. Princess Anne and Goodwill came a real 'cropper' at a vast 'bogey' fence when competing in the European Trials in Russia. When competing on the Olympic cross-country course in Canada, Goodwill slipped coming into a fence and they crashed again: the Princess was knocked out for a few minutes and can still remember nothing of riding and jumping on to the finish. On that occasion all the Royal Family were there to cheer her on, and although they were not standing by the fence in question, they saw the fall on closed-circuit television. It must have been a bad moment, though the Queen, as long as she knows that Anne has horses capable of what is required of them, would never dream of suggesting that her daughter modify her ambitions.

The Queen is unlikely again to go through all the excitements, and occasional anxieties, that Princess Anne's riding has brought her: competing with horses is not included in the pastimes of the younger Princes. The Queen taught Andrew and Edward the rudiments of riding and ponylore, and Edward still enjoys charging about on horseback on the estates, but although Andrew at the age of four was having fun with a little Shetland pony, his interest soon waned. It was not long before the familiar sound of hoofbeats on the gravel at Balmoral or Sandringham or Windsor was being superceded by the 'phut-phut' sound of go-karts as the boys and their cousins raced perilously round the corners or practised skid-turns to the detriment of the drive.

Andrew took up gliding a year or so ago and has now added flying to his accomplishments. He has also started parachuting, and, according to the photographer who has been present when both he and Prince Charles have landed, by their expressions both brothers find jumping out of planes an exhilarating pastime. As Prince Philip taught all the children to drive at an early age in the legitimate confines of the parks, no doubt Andrew combines driving skill with speed like the rest of the family. He too has chosen the Navy as a career and seems to have the same love of adventure for adventure's sake as his elder brother.

It is not excitement but tranquillity which the Queen craves. She is by nature a solitary person, and since much of her life is passed in the fullest glare of publicity, she needs more than most to get away by herself whenever she can. Every evening she walks for an hour or so with only her dogs for company. Despite the size of the gardens at Buckingham Palace, the near-by high-rise buildings now restrict her area of privacy, and at Windsor the peace of centuries has for years been shattered by the too frequent thunder and scream of great jets passing over to and from Heathrow Airport. At Balmoral there is little to disturb the tranquillity but the plaintive whistle of a curlew and sudden 'kok, kok, kok' as grouse fly up out of the heather. At Sandringham the woodland paths have a harmony of seclusion and bird-song of their own. But wherever the Queen may be, this evening walk is something she treasures.

Above Princess Anne and her husband Captain Mark Phillips are both top riders in the field of international horse trials. They became acquainted through this sport which continues to be of mutual interest now that they are married.

Below Prince Charles and Prince Andrew share the same love of adventure. Both enjoy jumping out of aeroplanes, although the Prince of Wales is a more advanced parachutist. The Princes are seen here during ground training.

7

Public Life

When the Queen first came to the throne, her own instinct of what was necessary for the monarchy at the time echoed the feelings of most of her subjects. They might be tired of the financial stringencies still evident seven years after the end of the war and might hail this 'new Elizabethan' era as the gateway to prosperity but basically they wanted the monarchy to remain much the same as it had been under George VI, the King they had had good reason to love and respect.

For Elizabeth, brought up to the tenets by which her grandfather and father ruled and lived, there seemed initially no reason for altering radically an institution which had survived the upheaval of the Abdication and, by returning to many of its former concepts, appeared to have become all the stronger. And this policy was adopted by the majority of the Queen's advisers, who were keeping a somewhat wary eye on Prince Philip, whom they suspected of being something of a 'new broom'.

But times change, opinions alter, and before very long the Queen, her husband and her advisers had come to realize that, to survive, even an institution as traditional and honoured as the monarchy has to change too. It is a policy that began slowly and with restraint and still continues today, but the problem has always been to determine how far to go. Too little change, and the monarchy could become outmoded and out of touch; too much, and it could become commonplace or lose the values that provide its abiding stability.

In the mid-1950s, this balance was put to the test within the Royal Family itself, when Princess Margaret announced that she wished to marry a divorcé, Group Captain Peter Townsend. The Abdication furore of 1936 had not changed the Church of England's attitude to the remarriage of divorcés, but now, some twenty years after that crisis, public opinion, the voice of 'the man in the street', demanded a more liberal outlook. The question of the Princess's marriage, which was essentially a private matter for discussion within the Royal Family, was turned into a public debate largely because she was third in the line of succession.

Group Captain Peter Townsend DSO DFC was sixteen years Princess Margaret's senior and had known her since she was a child, having been her father's equerry from 1944 until 1950, when he was made Deputy Master of the Royal Household.

Opposite *The Queen and Prince Philip leaving St Paul's Cathedral after the annual service of the Order of St Michael and St George – an ancient order of chivalry named after two saints renowned for slaying dragons.*

Princess Margaret with Group Captain Peter Townsend in 1953, the man she loved but renounced – because he was a divorcé and she was 'Mindful of the Church's teaching that Christian marriage is indissoluble . . .'

Thus Margaret and Peter Townsend saw each other almost daily, and even while the popular Press was coupling the Princess's name with this or that scion of the aristocracy, she and Townsend were falling in love. After his divorce came through, at the end of 1952, the possibility of marriage was in the air.

But under the Royal Marriages Act of 1772 members of the Royal Family under the age of twenty five could not marry without the sovereign's consent. It posed a cruel dilemma for Queen Elizabeth, who obviously cared very much about her sister's personal happiness, but the law obliged her to act on the advice of her Prime Minister. To Winston Churchill such a marriage at that time was unthinkable. It was coronation year; it was the beginning of a new reign; and it would be disastrous for the Queen's only sister to marry a divorcé.

It was agreed that the Princess should wait two years until she was twenty five and more or less free to make up her own mind. The Queen withstood her ministers' wishes to send Townsend abroad and insisted that he remained in attendance at Clarence House, but Princess Margaret sabotaged this concession by her indiscreet behaviour after the coronation service. She was in love with the Group Captain and did not care who knew it. The rumours had already begun to fly, here was apparent confirmation and the British press began to comment on what 'must be an impossible story'. Townsend realized that he had to go away and in July 1953 was sent to take up a position as Air Attaché at the British Embassy in Brussels.

Peter Townsend and Princess Margaret were apart for more than two years, but when he returned to Britain, they found that nothing had changed between them. They knew the problems they faced in wanting to marry: the Anglican Church condemned the remarriage of divorcés – and Margaret's sister was the titular Head of the Anglican Church, bound to uphold its precepts.

While the Queen consulted with the elders of the Royal Family and with her ministers, arrangements were made for the Group Captain to stay with friends of the Queen, at whose house, suitably chaperoned, he and Margaret could meet. The plan was discreet and private, but within hours every move was being reported in the popular Press. As the rumours spread, the furore increased. Many people simply refused to believe that a member of the Royal Family could be contemplating a marriage that went so directly against their own moral code and the teaching of the Church; at the other pole, however, there were many to declare 'All for love and the world well lost'.

The issues, as seen by a leader-writer in *The Times*, were plain: either the Queen's sister would be 'entering into a union which vast numbers ... cannot in conscience regard as a marriage' or she must make a sacrifice in the cause of duty. The Government's reaction to the Princess's wishes was that, if she contracted the marriage, she would have to renounce her rights to the throne and her official income, and retire into private life out of the country.

On 31 October 1955 Princess Margaret issued a statement: 'Mindful of the Church's teaching that Christian marriage is indissoluble, and conscious of my duty to the Commonwealth, I have resolved to put these considerations before any others. . . .'

Princess Margaret's sacrifice was made all the more tragic, in retrospect, in view of her own divorce. But by that time the monarchy had already accommodated itself to the break-down of the marriage of one of its members, the Queen's cousin the Earl of Harewood in 1967. Prime Minister Wilson rescued the Queen on that occasion, from the dilemma of making a decision as Head of the Church, by consulting with his Cabinet and 'advising' her to show indulgence to the wish of Lord Harewood to remarry. Times had changed since Princess Margaret's sad conflict of love and duty.

It is not clear how far the controversy of the Margaret/Townsend affair was responsible for a temporary decline in the popularity of the monarchy, but a decline there was, especially noticeable in the carping tone of the popular Press. For some months in 1957 there appeared well-publicized attacks on the Queen's personal advisers (as being reactionary diehards, employed more by reason of their blue blood than for their intellect) and some criticism of the Queen herself.

Fair or not, the outcome of criticism can be constructive. In 1957 it was healthier and perhaps in the long term more beneficial to the monarchy than the fulsome adulation of earlier years. And, not perhaps coincidentally, changes were on the way. Parliament voted to create life peerages for men and women, enabling those without hereditary titles to sit and vote in the House of Lords, a constitutional amendment to which the Queen's support was all but essential. Less seriously, but still a sign of the times, the chapel at Buckingham Palace, bombed in the war, was

rebuilt, at the instigation of the Queen and Prince Philip, as 'The Queen's Gallery', where exhibitions of the royal art treasures were opened to the general public in 1962. Though most of the ceremonial and glitter, etiquette and protocol of past centuries was retained to serve the purpose for which they exist, such as ensuring that all ambassadors receive exactly the same treatment, from 1957 high-society girls no longer made their debut at exclusive presentation-parties at the Palace, and some of the more traditional balls and levées were replaced with informal luncheons and cocktail-parties for interesting people from all walks of life. Today explorers, astronauts, engineers, industrial barons, trades union leaders, writers, teachers and artists figure among the eight thousand guests at the three annual

Left *The royal garden parties, now encompassing a very wide spectrum of British and overseas guests, sprang originally from functions designed by Queen Victoria to present her vast clan of children and grandchildren to society's uppercrust.*

Above right *The Queen, accompanied by showbiz impresario Lord Grade, meets the all-star cast of the 1977 Silver Jubilee Royal Variety Gala which she and Prince Philip attended at the London Palladium. Enjoying a joke with Shirley Maclaine and Rudolf Nureyev.*

Below right *Holyrood House, once the palace of the kings of Scotland, now the Queen's residence in Edinburgh.*

garden-parties at Buckingham Palace (and one at Holyroodhouse) held each year. Once morning-dress (grey tail-coats and top-hats for men, a formal outfit with hat and gloves for women) was *de rigueur* at such functions; in the new, informal atmosphere, guests were recommended to wear whatever they themselves found suitable.

Among the less serious criticisms, at one stage the Queen was chided by the Press for looking too solemn at a Trooping the Colour, her official birthday parade. But her concept of her correct bearing as Head of State does not include a film-star smile; she is not playing a part. The dignity she shows riding to Horseguards Parade, and then taking the salute, is entirely fitting to the occasion. It is a different matter

Prince Edward's introduction to that well-known royal view from the balcony at Buckingham Palace. This picture was taken after the Queen's official birthday parade in 1964.

132

when the Queen and her horse are practising side-saddle in the covered school at Buckingham Palace during the weeks beforehand, when there is plenty of laughter at the jokes flying around. In the inner quadrangle of the Palace, where the Queen mounts to go to the ceremony, the atmosphere is relaxed and cheerful – until the demanding moment when she rides out in advance of her escort under the central archway into the forecourt and then onto the Mall, where the cheering builds up into an almost tangible barrier of emotional sound.

The Queens maintains a nice balance between the natural dignity she brings to her duties as head of state, and the equally natural human touches her former shyness tended to conceal. This is one outcome of a very happy, lively marriage, in which two people of very different temperaments have worked together through the years to make a rewarding, complementary partnership. One of the Queen and Prince Philip's greatest assets is that they are exceptionally good friends; another is that they share an endearing sense of the ridiculous, a saving grace for those whose life is spent principally in the public eye. (The Queen obviously enjoyed an amusing moment during the Persian Gulf tour of 1979, when a gust of the unpredictable Oman wind seized her hat during the playing of the national anthem. In a Moslem country it is certainly 'not done' for a woman to bare her head, but a quick clutch followed by a firm hold on the hat's brim saved the situation, and years of training saved the Queen's composure. The joke was obviously being shared with the young Sultan Qaboos bin Said as the two monarchs walked away.)

One criticism of the Queen, as unfair then as it would be today, concerned the so-called dullness of some of her official speeches, but it was based on a misconception of her role. The larger part of the Queen's work is done as 'Head of State', in which

The Queen holds firmly on to her hat in defiance of a gust of Oman wind! A moment captured by a Press photographer during the Persian Gulf tour.

Above *The Queen, Prince Philip, Prince Charles, Princess Anne and Captain Mark Phillips at the Commonwealth State Opening of Parliament.*

Right *The glorious spectacle of the State Opening of Parliament in the House of Lords. The Queen reads the Speech from the Throne, outlining the government's policies for the new Parliamentary Session.*

capacity she has to ensure that every speech she makes is phrased in accordance with existing government policy, with the Minister concerned allowed an opportunity to comment on its content. Thus, if the subject-matter of her speeches happens to be a little weighty and the words not entirely her own, it is scarcely the Queen's fault if the end-product does not scintillate, especially since she must prepare and deliver dozens of speeches every year.

Every country has to have a Head of State, whether monarch or president, and one of the duties of a Head of State is to perform the traditional, usually colourful and always time-consuming ceremonial which goes with that high office. The Queen, as hereditary Head of State, is thus able to free the elected leader of her government, her Prime Minister, to get on with the business of government, at the same time answering the continuing demands of the majority of her subjects (and thousands of foreign tourists to Britain) for the traditional glamour and romance of royal days long gone.

All day long, year in year out, people stand and stare through the gilt-topped railings across the forecourt to the imposing façade and some of the thousand windows of Buckingham Palace. Each morning (except for Sunday), the crowd

Above *The Queen enjoys driving in the privacy of her own grounds.*

Opposite *The Queen and Prince Philip arrive with Prince Edward at Westminster Abbey for their Silver Wedding anniversary service. On all official occasions the Queen is driven in her state Rolls-Royce.*

swells to fill and overflow the road between the railings and the Victoria Memorial to watch, at 11 a.m. precisely, the colourful, meticulously drilled Changing of the Guard. Those who arrive early have the bonus of seeing a contingent of Household Cavalry, the Life Guards one morning, the Blues and Royals the next, jingling by *en route* to Horseguards Parade to provide the four 'boxmen' who, two by two, mount guard at Whitehall.

Early or late visitors may see the small, single-horse carriage which calls twice a day to collect and deliver the royal mail that goes by hand. Sometimes there is the excitement of the arrival of a new ambassador to the Court of St James's, come to present his credentials to the Queen and traditionally conveyed to her palace in King Edward VII's Town Coach. Cars and some pedestrians go in and out of Buckingham Palace past the police-post at the entrance nearest to Constitution Hill. Now and again a car coming out of the North Centre Gate may provide the lucky few with a glimpse of Prince Philip, or of Prince Charles or Princess Anne at the wheel of their own sleek and speedy sports-cars, or it might be the Queen, being driven out in one of her four maroon and black Rolls Royces, on her way to some official engagement.

And of all the millions who through the years stop to stand and stare, some may know that if the royal standard is not flying over the Palace roof, then the Queen is

not at home, and that the Queen's absence is also denoted by the presence of 'the Short Guard' (a smaller contingent of Household Cavalry than when the Queen is in residence), who trot straight by the Palace without pausing for the trumpeter to sound a salute. But few among those waiting crowds have any real idea of what goes on behind the big doors of Buckingham Palace.

Like Windsor Castle and the Palace of Holyroodhouse in Edinburgh, Buckingham Palace is Crown property – that is, not the sovereign's personal property but held 'in trust' from the nation. The magnificent state apartments filled with priceless works of art (also state-owned and including nearly twenty thousand paintings and drawings, most of them on show to the public in the Queen's Gallery) are the perfect setting for the ceremonies for which they were designed: state balls where the jewels and tiaras and decorations out-sparkle the chandeliers, and state banquets where the dinner-service is of solid silver, or gold for even more splendid occasions. The 'diplomatic evening' in November, when representatives from all the foreign embassies and high commissions are received, involve more than a hundred countries and over a thousand guests, and are the only occasions on which all nine state rooms are in use at the same time. For the dozen or so investitures which the Queen holds each year, the grand ballroom at the Palace is used. Some two thousand men and women come here each year to receive titles and decorations, usually awarded for services to the nation and the Commonwealth, but some of the honours the Queen hands out, those of the Royal Victorian Order, are in her personal gift and may be given with less formality at Balmoral or Sandringham.

"Hang on, sir . . . my mistake . . . you're Admiral of the Fleet today!"

The Queen spends most of the year at Buckingham Palace, living in the royal apartments, which, in contrast to the splendours of the ceremonial rooms, are simple and 'homey'. But in addition to being a home, Buckingham Palace is, of course, the Queen's working centre. Every morning at ten o'clock her private secretary comes with the morning's mail to the Queen's office (next to that of her husband). The Queen's daily post is enormous. Besides official documents, she receives a multitude of letters from 'ordinary' people: sad letters, admiring letters, complaining letters, funny ones, requests for help in personal tragedy, entreaties for support over quarrels with officialdom and a few that are unashamedly begging. The Queen answers letters from friends herself in her own hand; all the others, with the possible exception of those from obvious cranks, are dealt with by the royal secretaries and her ladies-in-waiting; those involving administrative or political questions are usually sent on to the appropriate government department for the necessary inquiries to be made.

Every morning the Queen spends several hours reading through and signing the state papers which arrive each day in the famous 'red boxes', wherever she may be.

The Queen and Prince Philip walk in procession to
St George's Chapel, Windsor, for the installation of the
Knights of the Garter, the oldest order of English chivalry.

They include the most important Cabinet papers, Foreign Office telegrams and dispatches and those from Commonwealth High Commissioners, and a daily summary of Parliament's proceedings, in addition to the verbatim Hansard report. The Queen reads quickly but studying and absorbing all the outstanding points in each document (her thoroughness was once an embarrassment to Winston Churchill when he was questioned about an item he had failed to read himself). In this way the Queen is always up to date with the nation's most important business and with Commonwealth and world affairs. Churchill, tongue in cheek, used to say he and the Queen chiefly discussed racing. She developed a particularly good and easy working relationship with Harold Macmillan. Harold Wilson got off to an unprecedented start – by taking his wife, father and sister to the Palace when he kissed hands on his appointment. Whatever their pre-conceived ideas, all the Queen's ministers who work with her succumb to her friendly, professional approach. The late Richard Crossman, who disliked court 'flummery' on principle, when made Lord President of the Council unwittingly confided to a friend of the Queen's that he found his sovereign 'frightfully horsey'. At their first official meeting at Buckingham Palace soon after, Crossman, stiff and ill at ease, was bowled over when the Queen remarked sweetly: 'I hear you had dinner with ——— the other evening?', and smiled, the merest glint of mischief in her eye.

Apart from her traditional weekly meeting with her Prime Minister, the Queen is entitled to discuss with her ministers the business of their respective departments. She can, and does, give her own views, advising, encouraging and occasionally warning – and she has gained the respect of all her Prime Ministers for the considered good judgement of her opinions. And since, through the years, the Queen has had the opportunity to accumulate an uninterrupted knowledge of the inner workings of government and to know many British political figures, foreign statesmen and Commonwealth leaders, she is well-equipped to give opinions on national and international trends, passing on her experience where it is relevant. Governments change, but the Queen is always there, acquiring and applying a knowledge and wisdom which are invaluable.

When her work on national affairs is finished for the day, or set aside until the evening, the Queen still has many things to discuss with her private secretary, matters that may range from checking the programme for some forthcoming tour

Opposite above *The Queen and Prince Philip entertaining the seven world leaders in London for the two-day Downing Street summit talks in 1977. From left to right: Pierre Trudeau (Canada), Takeo Fukuda (Japan), Princess Margaret, James Callaghan, Prince Charles, Giscard d'Estaing (France), HM Queen Elizabeth II, HM Queen Elizabeth the Queen Mother, Jimmy Carter (USA), Giulio Andreotti (Italy), Prince Philip and Helmut Schmidt (West Germany).*

Opposite below *A selection of bank notes issued by various Commonwealth countries, each showing a different portrait of the Queen.*

abroad to approving official appointments or names recommended for honours. Her secretary is her right-hand man, the principal liaison officer between the Palace and the Government, a man usually to be found wherever the Queen may be, but unobtrusively in the background. His department heads the five which help the Queen run the monarchy and Palace.

The Master of the Household is most important in the domestic sphere, and there is usually plenty to discuss with him. He is responsible for everything in the royal households from the correct setting of the table for a banquet to new arrangements for the comfort of the domestic staff. His responsibilities remain the same whether the Queen is at Buckingham Palace or at Windsor, Sandringham, Balmoral or Holyroodhouse; about a hundred of the London staff are moved from one royal residence to another as required.

The normal round of royal work is sufficient to keep the officers and staff of the Queen's household very fully occupied. The various departments, whose offices are on the ground floor of Buckingham Palace, are integrated and complementary to each other, the over-all atmosphere relaxed and friendly, with a light-hearted camaraderie which is infectious and, as in most well-run business associations, emanates from the top. They are linked via the intercom system that was among the first of Prince Philip's modernizations, and sometimes the conversations over this indispensible means of communication are not as serious as might be imagined.

Consultations with the officers of her household completed, the Queen may receive the first of her visitors. She gives two or three hundred audiences a year, often five in a day, maybe to a bishop or a new ambassador, to a Cabinet minister relinquishing office or a member of the diplomatic corps taking up a new appointment. Many of her visitors are from the Commonwealth countries.

Sitting to an artist or photographer is something the Queen often has to fit into her day. And because, wherever she is and whatever she is doing, her appearance must be right for the occasion, she has to spend considerably more time with her hairdresser and dressmaker than she would otherwise choose to. By keeping more or less to the skirt length dictated by current fashion but retaining the line and style that she likes and finds most appropriate, the Queen's clothes seldom 'date'. And with the colours she prefers, clear blues and greens, lemon yellow, lavender, sometimes pinks or browns, it is possible to do some clever 'mixing and matching'. Her clothes for foreign tours have to be planned months in advance, with an eye to whatever season it will then be.

Every year the Queen receives literally thousands of invitations to visit hospitals and schools, institutions and factories, in every part of the British Isles. She inspects regiments, occasionally plants a commemorative tree – and lets it be known that she would much rather visit a going concern than lay a foundation-stone. With the aid of her advisers, each suggestion, bar the obviously impracticable, is carefully considered and as many as possible squeezed into the yearly round. But although

Opposite: *A fine photographic portrait of HM Queen Elizabeth II by Cecil Beaton, 1968.*

The Queen wears a variety of charming hats in a variety of vibrant colours, but all share the royal requirement to be 'off the face'.

Above *The Queen attired in headscarf and pit helmet for descending a coal-mine.*

the Queen's and Prince Philip's diaries of engagements are always full, and working independently for part of the time enables them to do that much more, the number of invitations they can accept (usually the Queen averages about a hundred a year) is nothing compared with those which sheer lack of time forces them to refuse.

One curious aspect of the royal working day is that although the family thoroughly enjoys its engagements together, and family matters are always fully discussed, the public functions they perform separately quite often get left out of the conversation. Then it suddenly transpires in their various offices that the family is totally unaware of one another's assignments!

Since her accession there have been only two years in which the Queen has not received foreign royalty or presidents on state visits to Britain, and these occasions involve the most meticulous planning. But the extra work they demand is nothing compared with that required for a state visit or royal tour by the Queen.

The success of such occasions depends mainly on the personality, good sense and downright stamina of the principals, plus co-ordinated arrangements down to the last detail by those responsible for operating the agreed programme. On the first

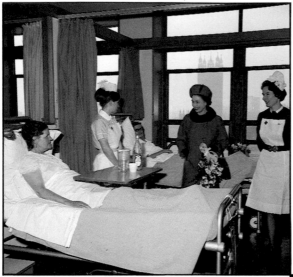

Visiting the sick is a royal engagement that the Queen counts as a priority. Here she visits St Thomas's Hospital.

In 1969 the Queen opened the new section of the Victoria Line Underground. Ten years later Prince Charles was performing the same royal duty for the Jubilee Line at Green Park.

The Queen, brought up by 'gardening' parents, enjoys the colour and beauty of Chelsea Flower Show.

count the Queen and Prince Philip certainly acquit themselves well, and bar the occasional small miscalculation due to unforseen circumstances, those in charge of the tours do the same. The Queen's undoubted diplomatic skill lies chiefly in her ability to put people at ease and a sense of humour produced at unexpected moments. An embarrassed British ambassador, attempting to put across politely the eccentricities of a foreign head of government, was helped by the Queen inquiring: 'Are you trying to tell me that the man is just bonkers?' But she chooses her moments. When an unfortunate foreign ambassador slipped and fell at her feet the Queen looked furious – but her expression was entirely owing to her valiant efforts not to laugh and put him to shame.

The idea that the Royal Family should strengthen the throne and set an example by the character and behaviour of its various members, started to emerge only during the Victorian era. Today, as Prince Philip says, one of the assets of the monarchy is that it does involve a whole family, with different age groups to which people can look and identify. And certainly the Queen is thankful for the help and support of various members of her family, principally in carrying out ceremonial duties overseas and some of the innumerable visits to various parts of Britain.

Prince Philip is of course the Queen's chief assistant, and her complement too: the things she finds difficult (such as off-the-cuff speech-making) are some of those that her husband does best, and the things about which he gets impatient are those that she will take the time and trouble to work out.

Nowadays Prince Charles also helps take an annually greater part of the load off the Queen's shoulders, in addition to fulfilling his own commitments as Prince of Wales. In earlier years Prince Charles accompanied the Queen and Prince Philip on some of their royal tours, to New Zealand and Australia, to Canada, including 'the frozen north', and on a state visit to France. During his years in the Royal Navy he was able to undertake a number of overseas duties in his 'ambassadorial' role, and he looks on Australia almost as a second home. Increasingly he represents the Queen abroad, as in his exhaustive and exhausting tour of the United States in 1977, of Brazil and Venezuela in 1978, and a year later in Yugoslavia, his first visit to a Communist, if non-aligned, country. Early in 1979 his tour of the Far East was one of the longest he has undertaken to date. Sometimes he attends the independence day celebrations of some former colony, such as Fiji in 1970, and the Bahamas in 1973. Wherever the Prince goes, his ease and charming manner earn him a rapturous welcome, and as he gets older and his tours become more extensive, the message he brings of the Queen's continuing interest is carried farther afield. And the more he travels the world and learns of its different peoples, the better qualified he becomes for his future rôle as monarch. In the meantime, at home or abroad, the Queen is finding her eldest son an invaluable and immensely popular member of 'the royal firm'.

Princess Anne, Mrs Mark Phillips, fourth in the line of succession, is another active member of the 'firm'. When she was younger and first embarking on serious

A happy royal wedding party came out to see the crowds, massed in front of the Palace, after the wedding of Princess Anne and Captain Mark Phillips on 14 November 1973.

competitive riding, some public 'advisers' suggested that she should be 'let off' her public duties, but, as frequently happens, the pundits were missing the point: the Princess sometimes used to kick a little against the limitations of her life; like her father she did not rate the ability to 'open things' well as a particularly gainful achievement; but Anne has always been very conscious that her great-grandfather, George v's, saying: 'We're not a family, we're a firm,' is as true of her generation as it was of his. It was never part of the Princess's nature to opt out of her share of the obligations. She is always ready to help her mother, for whom she has the deepest love and admiration. In 1978 Princess Anne, either on her own or with her husband, fulfilled fifty-two public engagements – a good contribution to the 'firm's' work.

Now that the Princess is happily married, with her own home and family, it is Prince Charles who more often hits the headlines, but the Princess is still deeply concerned with her two main public interests, Riding for the Disabled and enterprises concerning children (she is President of the Save the Children Fund). And now that Mark Phillips has left the Army to concentrate on farming, projects concerning the land are starting to figure on the list of public functions they attend together.

The Queen and Prince Philip have continued, with the two younger boys, their policy of trying to give their family a normal childhood. In fact, despite the

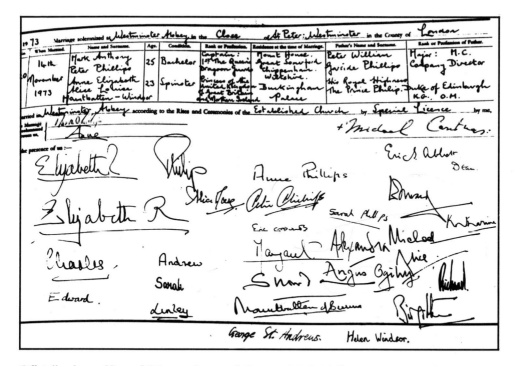

Officially the wedding of Princess Anne and Captain Mark Phillips was a private family affair, but the occasion was watched by a world-wide television audience of 500,000,000. There was also a galaxy of royal signatures on the marriage certificate.

pressures, they have succeeded in keeping them all in the background when young, to a far greater extent than was achieved, or even attempted, when the Queen and Margaret were children in the 1930s. Prince Charles's face was familiar to the public, but he himself was almost unknown until his investiture as Prince of Wales. At that ceremony, held at Caernarvon Castle in 1969, Charles knelt before his mother, put his hand in hers and promised: 'I, Charles, Prince of Wales, do become your liege man of life and limb, and of earthly worship . . .' Thereafter he made a start on public engagements as part of the royal team. Prince Andrew, more extrovert than his brothers, is already acquiring a public 'persona', and in due time Prince Edward, despite the fact that he is known to be quiet and retiring, will be drawn into the limelight and into public duties too.

With the exception of her husband, of all her family the Queen has had the most help from Queen Elizabeth the Queen Mother. After the death of her husband, King George VI, she had become very depressed and 'lost', but, with her daughters' help and her own strength of character, Queen Elizabeth confronted her loss in the way she knew her husband would have wished – together they had never run away from anything that had to be faced. In a message to the nation, she declared that she wished to be allowed to continue 'the great task of service that was laid upon us', supporting and backing up the new Queen in every way she could. And that is what

Left *The poignant moment during the ceremony at Caernarvon Castle when the Queen invested Charles as Prince of Wales.*

Right *The Queen Mother in the garden at Clarence House, her London home, on her seventieth birthday. She was visited by some of her grandchildren – Prince Edward, Viscount Linley and Lady Sarah Armstrong-Jones.*

the Queen Mother has been doing with much energy and enjoyment ever since. When she realized that there was a new and important role for her to fulfil as Queen Mother, she set about creating an indispensible and dynamic career for herself. It is one that bears little resemblance to the position of Dowager Queen as interpreted by Queen Alexandra and Queen Mary.

All her life she has been blithe, amusing, often witty. She was born with a natural charm and genuine interest in other people which her grandson, Charles, has inherited; her sense of fun matches that of the other members of the family. She was beloved as a queen, and the affection and admiration people feel for her has increased with the years.

With her daughter's accession it would have been much regretted, but understood, if the Queen Mother, after nearly half a lifetime of public service, had decided to slow down a little. But more than a quarter of a century later she is still showing no signs of doing so and is making few if any concessions to age.

Since 1953, when she flew in a Comet with Princess Margaret to Rhodesia, the Queen Mother has been jetting happily about the Commonwealth, revisiting Canada and Australia and accepting an invitation to the United States. She made a world tour in 1958 and in the years since has visited Mauritius, Kenya, Nyasaland, Italy, Tunisia and Sardinia in her travels. She went off to New Zealand again in both

1966 and 1974 and occasionally takes a short holiday in France. In 1975 she was genuinely disappointed when a technical hitch prevented her flying in Concorde to Iran. If the Queen Mother's overseas engagements have lessened a little in the past few years it is principally because of the changing aspect of the Commonwealth.

Certainly her travelling less has not been matched by her taking fewer public engagements. When the Queen is away, her mother acts as senior Counsellor of State, taking investitures, holding councils and helping deal with official papers. The year of the Silver Jubilee, 1977, was one of the Queen Mother's busiest. Two years later her 'operational day' was still beginning at 10.30 a.m. and continuing until 1 p.m., and most afternoons, if there is nothing further afield, there is a local engagement – that is, one within twenty miles of London; a glance at the Court Circular often depicts her participating at the Royal Family's evening commitments too.

The Queen Mother is voted a 'super' grandmother by her six grandchildren (she has always had a specially close relationship with Prince Charles), and her great-grandson Peter Mark Phillips is now an additional source of joy. Mother and daughters are very close, and whenever possible the Queen's day starts with a long telephone call to Clarence House.

The Queen will often also make a morning call to Princess Margaret.

Occasionally in the past these conversations have taken place at moments when the Queen's anxiety about her sister has matched the Princess's need for sympathy. Life has not been over-kind to Margaret, still seeking a worthwhile identity for herself, and the fact that what goes wrong is sometimes the outcome of her own actions makes it no easier for her.

On her wedding day, 6 May 1960, when a part of the Mall, the processional route to Westminster Abbey, was spanned by a high framework supporting garlands of roses, it seemed that Princess Margaret was heading for fulfilment and happiness with Antony Armstrong-Jones, a talented photographer soon to be created Earl of Snowdon. She was intensely in love with her husband and intensely possessive. In a situation that bore no resemblance to it, she wanted their married partnership somehow to reflect that of the Queen and Prince Philip.

For a while the Snowdons carried out a number of royal engagements together, but 'Tony' was a creative man used to earning his own living, and his attempt at combining royal duties with an unpaid job as consultant to the Design Centre did not succeed. He became a salaried artistic adviser to *The Sunday Times*'s colour supplement and gradually began using his talents in other ways besides photography – creating a new type of invalid chair, making very successful documentary

Princess Margaret on her wedding day, 6 May 1960.

films and usually letting his wife cope with their royal commitments. His was a successful career, but the marriage was rapidly becoming less successful. Both the Princess and the Earl were highly strung, strong willed and difficult, and their disagreements were not confined to the privacy of their own home. Before very long their social lives had become as separate as their public ones.

Under the moderated divorce laws of 1967, a straightforward dissolution of the marriage became possible after an agreed separation of two years. This was what the Princess and her husband wanted, but they decided to postpone the separation until the children were old enough to go away to school.

In the early 1970s the gossip columns were increasingly carrying stories of the Snowdons' separation, and by 1976 the Press had begun commenting on their separate life-styles. The official separation was therefore speeded up and announced on 19 March that year, and the divorce was finalized two years later.

Throughout the years of personal difficulties Princess Margaret has continued to fulfil some royal engagements and a glance at the Court circular now will show her daily attending two or three engagements as a royal representative.

In addition to her immediate family the Queen has a number of other relatives who can be called on as part of the team. This is particularly helpful in providing a more extensive cross-section of age-groups and interest, and as substitutes when illness or childbirth or anything else puts another member temporarily out of action.

The Queen's aunt by marriage, Princess Alice, Duchess of Gloucester, is still actively engaged in public duties, as are her son and daughter-in-law, the Duke and Duchess of Gloucester. The Duke of Kent, no longer serving with the Army and busy making a career in exports, includes royal engagements as part of his life, and the Duchess of Kent is also a hard-working member of the royal team.

It was a great relief to the Queen when her cousin, Princess Alexandra, (sister of the Duke of Kent), became old enough to start helping, in the days when the family team was not as extensive as it is today. In 1963 Alexandra married Angus Ogilvy, a business man who preferred to keep his marriage an essentially private alliance. They appear in public together on the kind of engagements that would normally concern a married couple, and when the Princess goes abroad to represent the Queen her husband usually accompanies her. Otherwise, whenever she can, Princess Alexandra willingly undertakes any royal engagement asked of her, and with her natural, sparkling personality is one of the most popular members of the Royal Family. Her younger brother Prince Michael of Kent had to renounce his place in the succession to the throne when he married the Austrian Baroness Marie-Christine von Reibnitz in June 1978, because she is a Roman Catholic, but he is always ready to play his part when his Army duties allow.

As most of the Queen's cousins now have children, as well as her sister, she will soon have quite a crowd of the younger generation to employ in various capacities in the royal firm.

8

A Modern Monarch

In 1977, the year of her Silver Jubilee, Queen Elizabeth undertook the most extensive and prolonged programme of any sovereign to date.

The Jubilee proved to be an astonishing celebration of the first quarter-century of a reign during which the world, and many of the people in it, changed to an astonishing degree. Of all the monarchs and presidents and heads of state the Queen had known, entertained and been entertained by during those years, by 1977 at least twenty-four of them were gone: either dead, (some by assassination) or deposed, and one, President Nixon of the United States, had been obliged to resign. Trams were still running in London when the Queen came to the throne, but within four years the United States had launched the first earth satellite: in 1969 the Queen received the crew of *Apollo 11* at the Palace and listened to the first-hand stories of those first men to set foot on the moon. When the Royal Family first moved from the comforts of Clarence House to the rambling vastness of Buckingham Palace, some of the rooms there were still illuminated by one inadequate electric light bulb switched on in the passage outside, some of the heating provided by one bar of an antiquated electric fire: four years later the Queen opened Calder Hall, Britain's first nuclear power station, which, by the time of her Silver Jubilee, was feeding nearly 200,000 kilowatts of electricity into the national grid. In 1960 the Queen launched *HMS Dreadnought*, the first British nuclear submarine.

One of the most remarkable leaps forward in technology during that time, and one that most affected the Royal Family, was in the media. When the Queen first came to the throne, the tools used by the Press and cinema newsreels were relatively unsophisticated compared with modern equipment. It was only sixteen years before the Queen's accession that the BBC had inaugurated the first television service in Britain, but by 1962 the first television transmissions by satellite were being made.

In 1957 the Queen delivered her Christmas message on television for the first time. It is not a medium that she has ever found easy or enjoys very much, and as in those days videotape recordings were very poor, the talk had to be broadcast 'live' – a daunting prospect that must have considerably reduced the Queen's enjoyment of her Christmas lunch! Nowadays the Queen is a seasoned broadcaster, well used to the intrusive eye of the television camera following her every movement for at least

Opposite *The Queen arrives for a display of folk dancing beneath the magnificent water towers of Kuwait.*

part of the time on public occasions. She is on good terms with most of the photographers and movie-cameramen who move backwards, with a solid wall of clicking, often whirring machines, as she advances down a street. But it does add to the sheer physical stamina required of her on public occasions, to know that at every moment she is subject to the closest, clearest scrutiny by millions of viewers.

Nevertheless, the Queen also knows very well that this medium has brought her closer to her people than was ever possible in previous reigns. For millions of people television provides the opportunity to see and enjoy all the traditional pomp and magnificence of the great state ceremonies, and the more they see of her performing public duties, the more they want to know of her private life.

The Queen has a right to a life of her own, and the Royal Family's private life is, to an extent, still jealously guarded, but throughout the years the Royal Family has become increasingly reasonable about what is considered 'legitimate interest'. The very successful television programme *Royal Family*, filmed between June 1968 and May 1969, went a long way towards satisfying the numerous people who would like to imagine the Queen and Prince Philip sitting at home drinking a cup of tea. And since 1971 the Queen's televized Christmas message has come in a new form, part of it showing her with various members of her family – with the two younger boys, behind the scenes after coming indoors from the balcony on Princess Anne's wedding day, and in 1978 in her new role as grandmother to little Peter Phillips.

The main ambition of many editors is for their reporters or photographers to get a 'scoop', an 'exclusive' story or a photograph with a new angle. During the Jubilee one national newspaper decided that it was a time for a change from all the photographs of the Queen smiling and happy: she was doing so much she must be getting over-tired, he thought, and a photograph suggesting that the Queen was being overtaxed would make 'a new angle'. So a photographer was commissioned to get the required picture. It was not a very easy assignment, because, tired or not, the Queen was so obviously enjoying herself, but on one particular day there was a moment when she was intent on something, and as the Queen's features in repose can make her look rather solemn, the photographer got a close-up that, with the right caption, was just what his editor wanted.

Initially no one had any real idea of how the country would react to the Silver Jubilee, as during the early 1970s the monarchy had been going through another rather unpopular period. This time it was not personalities that were being criticized but costs: the monarchy is not immune to inflation, and it was 'in the red' by 1970, but a request for an increase in the Civil List sparked off a storm of protest from Parliament and surmises about the Queen's private fortune from some sections of the public. Harold Wilson, then Prime Minister, set up a Select Committee to examine the expenditure of the Civil List, which resulted in large increases as reimbursements for operating expenses, principally wage increases for the royal household staff, and it was made very plain that this could not possibly be

Opposite The Queen on a walkabout in Portsmouth, Hampshire, during her Silver Jubilee celebrations in 1977.

construed as an 'increase' for the Queen or any of her family. The arguments rumbled on for a while but had died down, for all but the extremists, by 1977. But could Jubilee celebrations, which much of the country might not want anyway, be considered a justifiable expense in a time of national stringency?

The Queen and her advisers gave a great deal of thought to the matter before coming up with a possible solution: the Queen herself and the members of the Royal Family would obviously have a planned programme, but the keynote of this jubilee should be informality. And as far as the country was concerned, except for the Queen's Silver Jubilee Appeal Fund, set up and launched in April 1977 by the Prince of Wales, to raise funds for helping young people to help others, to celebrate or not was for the people to decide.

On 22 February in Jubilee year, the Queen and Prince Philip arrived in Auckland, New Zealand, at the start of a two-week visit. In Wellington on 28 February the Queen read the Speech from the Throne at the opening of the second session of New Zealand's thirty-eighth Parliament; earlier that day she had conferred five knighthoods at an investiture in Wellington Town Hall; but those two ceremonies marked the end of most of the formal ceremonies. After that the Queen belonged to the crowds in the streets who came to greet her, and New Zealand set the scene for what was to come back home.

Between 17 May and 11 August, when the tour ended, she travelled through Scotland and across England, from Humberside and Yorkshire down to the

158

Opposite The Queen wears a ceremonial Maori cloak presented to her during the Jubilee tour of New Zealand.

Above On the first day of her extensive Jubilee tour of Scotland the Queen attended the England v. Scotland football match at Hampden Park in Glasgow, and met Kenny Dalglish and the other members of the Scottish team.

Midlands, east to Norfolk and Suffolk, south again right down to Cornwall, then west to Wales and across the sea to Northern Ireland. London had two separate tours, as well as the special four days that began with the Silver Jubilee Bank Holiday on Tuesday 7 June.

Everywhere in the length and breadth of the British Isles the response to the Jubilee was the same, a spontaneous outpouring of national enjoyment and displays of enthusiasm that took everyone, including the Queen, completely by surprise. It would be impossible to analyse that spirit of Jubilee which no one had expected and at which the anti-monarchists would have laughed in scorn if anyone had suggested the possibility beforehand. If there were any anti-monarchists about during the summer of 1977, they had good reason not to air their views, for if the popular mood owed something to an admirable excuse to forget the stringency of the times, it originated and flowered in the affection and admiration felt for the sincere, hard-working woman who had promised twenty-five years before to serve her people – and who has been doing so faithfully ever since.

The Queen's Silver Jubilee in 1977 was a time for fun rapturously welcomed by the British people, who celebrated with energy and enthusiasm up and down the country.

London was en fête for the celebrations.

Prince charles trying out a special Jubilee taxi, used in connection with the Queen's Silver Jubilee Appeal Fund.
Right The emblem commissioned by King George v's Jubilee Trust for The Queen's Silver Jubilee Appeal.

The gold state coach comes through the central archway en route from Buckingham Palace to St Paul's Cathedral.

Colourful golf umbrellas vie with the brilliance of the golden coach.

Many of the Jubilee souvenirs, like this Wedgwood mug, were of good design and colouring.

If you did not want to wave a Union Jack you could wear it on your head!

Jubilee medals make a fine waistcoat.

Flags were put to many uses.

As the Queen surveyed the scene from the steps of St Paul's Cathedral, after arriving for the Jubilee Thanksgiving Service, perhaps she recalled the last time she arrived there in the gold state coach – for her Coronation.

There were four thousand street parties in London alone.

The Queen has greeted many crowds from the Palace balcony, but never one like the immense throng who came to cheer her and show their affection on Jubilee Day.

The four special days of celebration in London began with a Thanksgiving at St Paul's Cathedral on Jubilee Day, at which the crowds along the processional route were given their fill of the pageantry they had come to see. For the second time in the reign the great golden coach came swaying out of the centre gate of the Palace drawn by its eight-horse team of Windsor Greys. Prince Philip was in uniform as Admiral of the Fleet, and Prince Charles, riding behind, was in full dress uniform as Colonel-in-Chief of the Welsh Guards, but the Queen wore not a crown and robes of office but a plain pink silk crêpe outfit in keeping with the informality which she had decided must mark the festival.

During those Jubilee days there were traditional ceremonial duties: after the thanksgiving service the Queen lunched at the Guildhall and made a speech. She received the Commonwealth Heads of Government; took the salute at her Birthday Parade at Horse Guards; and there was a Garter Service at St George's Chapel, Windsor. But there was also a river progress up from Greenwich, to lunch on *Britannia* in the Pool of London, and then tea with the Archbishop of Canterbury at Lambeth, and in the evening, after the river fireworks, the crowds assembled in front of the Palace, all round the Victoria Memorial and back to the railings and to either side, covering the roads like a living carpet, to bring the Queen out on the balcony to hear their cheers.

The crowds received the Queen rapturously on her 'walkabouts' wherever she went: in London, round St Paul's on Jubilee Day, on the other two days of London tours, and on subsequent tours all over the country. And if the people loved it, so did she. When the Queen smiles, she smiles with her eyes as well as her lips, and there was a sparkle and gaiety about her that was infectious. When she laughs, she laughs with her whole face, and on the night of the firework display at Windsor she was happy and excited and radiating fun like a young girl. She enjoyed it all: the unprecedented flood of letters, greeting a million people who came out on one day to greet her, lighting the first of a chain of bonfires at Windsor, the fairytale procession of lighted carriages that brought her back to Buckingham Palace. She loved the exuberance of the children, the funny hats and the flags, the things people said to her, the armfuls of posies they thrust into her hands, meeting characters like the old lady who, aged ten, had greeted Queen Victoria. Above all the Queen loved the spontaneous feeling of national unity, and what she had never quite realized before, just how much her people love and admire her.

Since she came to the throne there have been only four years in which the Queen, accompanied by Prince Philip, has not made at least one, and usually two or three, state visits or royal tours abroad, in addition to annual tours of different parts of the British Isles. Elizabeth II is not only Queen of the United Kingdom and Northern

Above *As the daughter of one Naval officer and the wife of another, the Queen, on board the royal yacht 'Britannia', was in her element at the Spithead review of the Fleet during her Jubilee celebrations.*

Below *Since her accession to the throne the Queen has travelled to most regions of the world on state visits, to other nations and to the countries of the Commonwealth. In India in 1961.*

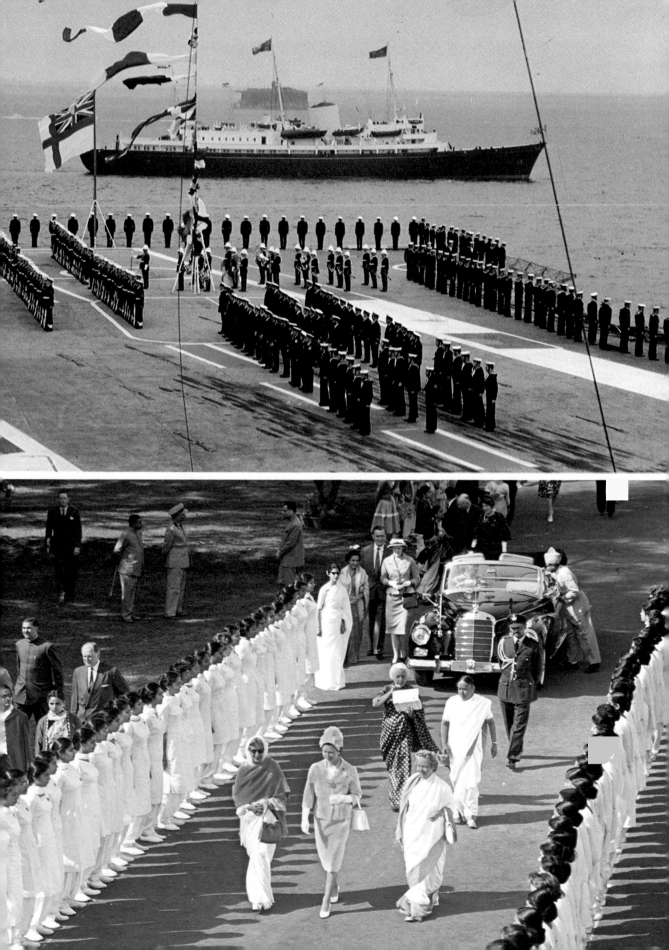

In 1979 the Queen and Prince Philip undertook an exhaustive and unprecedented tour of the Arab Gulf States. It was the first time a woman ruler had visited the man's world of the Gulf States.

Left *The Queen and Prince Philip's walkabouts in Eastern Arabia astonished and delighted the local populace.*

Above *The Queen honouring the Emir of Bahrain with the GCMG (Knight Grand Cross of St Michael and St George) at Qudaibiya Palace.*

Above right *Prince Philip chatting to a falconer in Bahrain.*

Right *The Queen and Prince Philip being greeted by King Khalid on arrival at Riyadh Airport at the start of their state visit to Saudi Arabia. The Queen wore a full-length blue silk ensemble as a diplomatic gesture.*

Ireland but also of realms and territories which include ten independent countries which have chosen to retain her as Head of State and of which she is Queen in her own right, besides being Head of the Commonwealth. Thus she visits as many of these countries as often as she can, making relatively frequent and lengthy tours to the old dominions of Canada, Australia and New Zealand.

On the post-Coronation tour which the Queen and Prince Philip undertook in the winter of 1953-54, they were away for 173 days and in Australia alone covered 13,400 miles by train, car and plane, a foretaste of gruelling tours to come. Aided by technological advance and the speed of modern transport, the Queen has become the most travelled monarch of all time. By 1977 she had carried out over fifty foreign tours involving more than a hundred countries.

The overseas tours are a very important part of the Queen's work, and those she and Prince Philip make to foreign countries help to strengthen friendly relations and economic ties. Although Prince Philip does not perhaps travel on his own quite as extensively as he once did, his journeyings all over the world are also of the greatest value. In the very early years the Queen realized that it would be impossible, and exhausting for all concerned, for someone of her husband's active, restless temperament to remain at home for too long at a time. Secure in their mutual affection, their personal partnership seems to have thrived on periodic partings, and their working partnership has also benefited to an enormous extent from Prince Philip's comings and going. His meetings, with people of every kind of background, ideology and race are something that the Queen cannot undertake, and they result in a huge fund of impressions, suggestions and information which make an invaluable contribution to the teamwork.

Apart from the Queen's triumphant African tour in August 1979, when the Commonwealth Conference included the controversial Zimbabwe–Rhodesia question, her three-week tour of six Arab countries earlier in 1979 could be the most important to date. It was planned many months before, and a meeting with the Shah of Iran was part of the schedule. When that section of the programme had to be cut owing to the Islamic revolution and the Shah's precipitate downfall, a tour originally conceived mainly as an exercise in the cause of British trade suddenly assumed much wider and more weighty implications. The majority of those oil-bearing countries, Kuwait, Bahrain, Qatar, the United Arab Emirates of Abu-Dhabi and Dubai, and powerful Saudi Arabia, were closely watching the turn of events across the Persian Gulf. As Iran's wells reduced oil-production for overseas markets, a consequent increase in price by the OPEC countries was made inevitable – though America's inability to save her powerful ally the Shah was of almost more consequence. The royal visit gave needed reassurance of continued friendship and interest to the hereditary Arab rulers, as well as strengthening economic ties.

The tour was considered an outstanding success. For the Queen, a woman ruler coming to an exclusively man's world, it was one of the most demanding, if one of the most interesting, she has undertaken.

XS789

Above *The Queen performed the State Opening of Parliament at Bridgetown, Barbados in 1977 – wearing the spectacles she now uses for reading.*

Sometimes a shifting political scene can suggest an element of danger to the Queen when she is about to travel abroad. But unless events, as in Iran, make her visit totally impracticable, the Queen is not easily persuaded from her objective by any fears for her safety. 'Danger', she told Harold Macmillan when he tried to stop her going to turbulent Ghana in 1961, 'is part of the job.' And those were no empty words: the Queen might have stopped a bullet intended for the unpopular President Nkrumah. She also toured French Canada in 1964, disregarding threats against her life. And up to the last feasible moment she had every intention of keeping her date with the Shah, if necessary on board *Britannia* anchored off Abadan.

The Royal Yacht, manned since the seventeenth century by the Royal Navy and at intervals the centre of criticism about maintenance costs, performs various functions. Sometimes, particularly in the past, the Royal Family have started their summer holiday by sailing up the west coast to Scotland – enjoying a few days of real freedom and seclusion at sea, as well as the famous hospitality of the Royal

Above *The royal yacht 'Britannia' serves many purposes, not least providing the Queen and Prince Philip with 'off duty' relaxation.*

Right *An impromptu water-ride much enjoyed by the Queen and her escort, Prince Henrik, in Copenhagen's Tivoli Gardens during her 1979 state visit to Denmark.*

Navy. *Britannia* is regularly used by the Navy on NATO exercises, but her most useful duty is as an extension of the Palace when the Queen is abroad. Usually the Queen flies in a VC 10 to her foreign commitments. She made the prestigious flight to the Arab countries of the Gulf in Concorde. (The three Andovers of the Queen's Flight are still used for relatively short journeys, principally by other members of the Royal Family and government ministers. Although sturdy and colourful, glistening in their red, white and blue paintwork, they have been in service for years and being turbo-props, have to fly at heights where turbulance can make trying to drink a cup of tea a hazardous undertaking. Prince Philip and Prince Charles frequently pilot these planes themselves.) On some state visits the Queen then joins *Britannia* as a prestigeous floating base for the remainder of the tour. This enables her to return hospitality to her hosts on a scale comparable to the Palace. On these occasions the Queen generally sleeps aboard ship to the immense relief of those responsible for her security.

"Honestly, Norman, I much preferred your collection for my American Tour!"

Umbrellas of State in lands overseas have differing significance and functions to those used for utilitarian purposes in Britain. Reading clockwise from left: The Queen in Thailand in 1972, in Nigeria in 1956, the British Virgin Islands in 1977 and during a wet drive in Australia!

Although the Queen has an innate personal courage, security is something she cannot disregard. It is an element of royal life with which she and her children grew up, and to which Prince Philip had to become accustomed. Princess Anne, schooling a pony in a field by herself when she was at Benenden, was approached by some workmen, who wanted to know if she realized that she was being watched by a large man smoking a pipe and leaning against a nearby building. When she showed no great surprise at the information (the man was her own detective-guard), she was then floored by the sceptical question: 'Huh . . . you a princess or something then?' But security is no joke in an era in which a politician can be assassinated by a bomb in the House of Commons car-park. And royal dangers have, of course, increased since the Queen instituted her very popular 'walk-abouts'.

Her first was in New Zealand during the Australasian tour of 1970. It was a great success in that country, but not so welcome in Australia where the security

arrangements are basically the concern of the different state governments: some of the security organizations found it very hard to adjust to the idea of the Queen walking down a street packed with a hundred thousand people, without the usual number of police and soldiers between her and those who had come to see her. In one or two places the police had to be positively encouraged not to stand shoulder to shoulder. In Brisbane, where they persisted, the Queen was adamant about doing the walk over again the next day, saying that there was simply no point in being able to talk only to policemen and soldiers.

Now, of course, the 'walkabouts' are an accepted and favourite aspect of all the Queen's tours at home or abroad, though in the Arab countries in 1979, where the populace are used to their rulers passing through as fast as the motorcade can go, the sight of the Queen and Prince Philip down among the crowds was as astonishing as the idea of a woman being a sovereign. (During that tour Prince Philip became separated from the royal party during one of the walkabouts. It was excessively hot, the crowd large and jostling, the noise inordinate, and the Queen invisible. The Prince is reported to have momentarily lost his temper and used some pithy expressions of disgust. But those who 'wrote to the papers' expressing their disapproval of such conduct showed little understanding of the normal reaction, under the circumstances, of a full-blooded man who believes in being himself and who spent twelve years in a navy not renowned for 'refined' euphemism.)

On any walkabout, time-schedules always preclude the Royal Family's chatting for more than a moment or two to any one person, but there is no doubt that the Queen really enjoys an opportunity to talk to anyone who catches her attention, to communicate with her subjects in a way unimaginable in any previous reign. But at the beginning it was not very easy for one of her reserved personality, and undoubtedly the ease with which her husband makes contact with people has helped the Queen to do the same. Time has helped too, like most of us the Queen has become more relaxed with age, more sure of herself. And no-one could spend hours of everyday life under the eye of a movie-camera, as the Royal Family did for the months of making the royal film, without becoming unselfconscious.

As for the bomb and assassination threats which, albeit stepped up in recent years, have always been one of the less pleasant aspects of royal life, the Royal Family take the only possible attitude – that as usual they will prove to be hoaxes. They always co-operate with any precautions the police think necessary, and then forget the danger and get on with the job.

Nevertheless it cannot be quite so easy to dismiss the threats since the 1974 attempt to kidnap Princess Anne, returning with Captain Mark Phillips to the Palace after an official engagement. The attempt took place in the Mall, where the assailant stopped the couple's car. While Mark Phillips was trying to stop his wife being pulled out of the car, the Princess's personal bodyguard was seriously wounded trying to shield her with his own body, and her elderly chauffeur was shot while grappling with the assailant. In all, four people were wounded while trying to help, and three others were lucky to escape injury. The bodyguard, a police inspector, received the George Cross for his gallantry, a constable and a civilian the George Medal, the Princess's chauffeur, another police constable and a passing journalist the Queen's Gallantry Medal, and another chauffeur who stopped to help, the Queen's Commendation for Brave Conduct. On the Princess's twenty-fourth birthday in August that year, '. . . to express her admiration of the Princess's calm and brave behaviour throughout the incident . . .', the Queen appointed her daughter a Dame Grand Cross of the Royal Victorian Order (GCVO). And 'to recognize the excellent conduct of Captain Mark Phillips and Miss Rowena Brassey' (the Princess's lady-in-waiting), she created her son-in-law a Commander (CVO) and Miss Brassey a Member of the Fourth Class (MVO).

Opposite *When the Queen laughs the world laughs with her.*

Afterword

It was during the year of the royal silver wedding anniversary that Prince Philip, reflecting on the stage of public life at which he and the Queen had arrived, suggested that it was an inbetween phase, no longer possessing the glamour of youth, not yet having attained the esteem due to age. And assessed purely by years, since the Queen was fifty-three in 1979 and her husband five years older, that is quite true. But no one could suggest that either of them is showing any signs of the 'stuffiness' and lessening of activity sometimes attributed to middle life.

Years ago the Queen gave up any attempt to make Prince Philip slacken off a little. If his staff are brave enough occasionally to make the suggestion, the Prince merely starts working out where he can possibly squeeze in another appointment. As for the Queen, in recent years, despite the good work of her eldest son, she seems to be increasing her assignments both at home and overseas.

The Queen now wears glasses for reading the Speech from the Throne at the State Opening of Parliament, and as a woman in her fifties it would be impossible for her face to show its former youthful bloom, but she has maintained her lovely complexion and trim figure. The Queen's face is that of a woman with a happy home life, and of one who still finds interest and fulfilment in a sometimes very exacting job. Of course there are many privileges and compensations attached to the monarchy, but her career is one that few would care to undertake. Apart from those innumerable everyday things which the Queen cannot do but which other people take for granted – such as going out alone at will, going where inclination suggests, it is sometimes forgotten that the Queen is humanly fallible. She does get tired, tense, occasionally irritable just like anyone else, but she is expected not to show it. The little laughter lines at the corners of her eyes suggest that, fortunately, she is someone who finds that her life, for all its ups and downs, usually has its funny side.

Like most families the Queen's is not immune from its quota of sadness and anxiety. Her uncle the Duke of Kent was killed on active service in 1942; her father's premature death was a tragedy; her cousin Prince William of Gloucester died in a flying accident in 1972. And in that same year the Queen went to see her uncle, the Duke of Windsor, in Paris, a week before he died. (For some years after Edward VIII's abdication there had been annual private meetings between the Queen and her uncle, and after the Duke of Windsor's death she showed compassionate thought

*The Queen and Prince Philip have found great happiness together – and have founded a
unique partnership, to their private contentment and the nation's good.*

for his widow, who came to Windsor for her husband's funeral. In the spring of
1979 all the Duke's private papers were collected from his Paris home and brought
back into the safe keeping of the Royal Archives at Windsor Castle.) In August
1979 the Queen had to face the atrocious murder by the Provisional IRA of Earl
Mountbatten of Burma, her cousin and Prince Philip's uncle and a man who spent
his long life in brilliant service to his country. The horrifying explosion which
shattered Lord Louis' boat also killed one of his grandsons and the Dowager Lady
Brabourne and seriously injured other members of his family. But in addition to
personal griefs and worries, the Queen has those of the nation to contend with, and
within hours of Mountbatten's tragic death she was informed of a similar explosion
close by over the border in Northern Ireland which killed eighteen British soldiers.

Since the Queen came to the throne in 1952 there have been many other national sorrows but there have of course been great achievements as well. Most of all there has been change, in countries and peoples and rulers. One subtle change for the Queen, unique in British history, was brought about by the new Conservative government in 1979, when Mrs Margaret Thatcher became Prime Minister – and with a queen regnant on the throne, another woman was now holding the position of executive power. But the greatest changes of all have come in human behaviour and thinking, with the increase of violence, new attitudes to sexual ethics and what constitutes public decency, and increasing materialism. Despite these changes the monarchy remains.

In this irreverent age the majority of people still respect simple virtues, which Elizabeth II, sincere, hard-working and down to earth, embodies. It is not easy to define exactly all the rights and duties of the monarchy, but one obvious service it supplies is in its traditional role as the symbol of a unified nation, not affected by the battle of party politics, a satisfactory focus for loyalty, an embodiment of tradition and history – a role which no transitory president can play. The Queen is also the shared link between members of the Commonwealth, binding them together not politically but in common ideals.

As for the future, a question raised at intervals is whether the Queen will abdicate in favour of Prince Charles: the Prince himself does not believe she will and sees no reason for it while his mother remains in good health. The Queen has ensured that her son sees a wide selection of state papers and is in every way learning the duties that will one day be his, but in the meantime Prince Charles is creating valuable work for himself in many different spheres, work that can be done only while he is heir to the throne, not on it. As it is, Britain is lucky enough to have a Prince of Wales who is doing an excellent job on his own and a Queen who provides every good reason for the majority of people in Britain still to consider a monarch the most satisfactory Head of State.

THE ROYAL HOUSE
OF WINDSOR

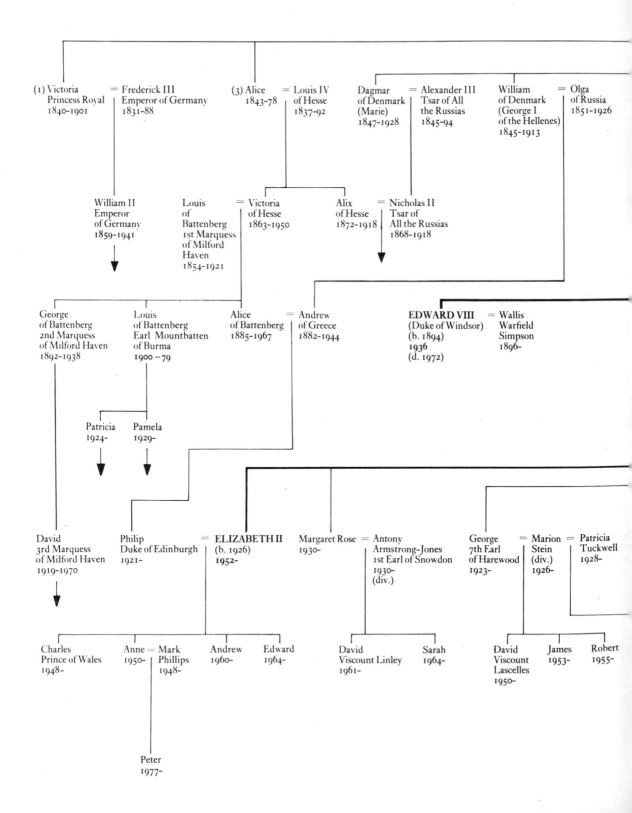

(1) Victoria
Princess Royal
1840-1901

= Frederick III
Emperor of Germany
1831-88

(3) Alice
1843-78

= Louis IV
of Hesse
1837-92

Dagmar
of Denmark
(Marie)
1847-1928

= Alexander III
Tsar of All
the Russias
1845-94

William
of Denmark
(George I
of the Hellenes)
1845-1913

= Olga
of Russia
1851-1926

William II
Emperor
of Germany
1859-1941

Louis
of
Battenberg
1st Marquess
of Milford
Haven
1854-1921

= Victoria
of Hesse
1863-1950

Alix
of Hesse
1872-1918

= Nicholas II
Tsar of
All the Russias
1868-1918

George
of Battenberg
2nd Marquess
of Milford Haven
1892-1938

Louis
of Battenberg
Earl Mountbatten
of Burma
1900 – 79

Alice
of Battenberg
1885-1967

= Andrew
of Greece
1882-1944

EDWARD VIII
(Duke of Windsor)
(b. 1894)
1936
(d. 1972)

= Wallis
Warfield
Simpson
1896-

Patricia
1924-

Pamela
1929-

David
3rd Marquess
of Milford Haven
1919-1970

Philip
Duke of Edinburgh
1921-

= **ELIZABETH II**
(b. 1926)
1952-

Margaret Rose
1930-

= Antony
Armstrong-Jones
1st Earl of Snowdon
1930-
(div.)

George
7th Earl
of Harewood
1923-

= Marion
Stein
(div.)
1926-

= Patricia
Tuckwell
1928-

Charles
Prince of Wales
1948-

Anne
1950-

= Mark
Phillips
1948-

Andrew
1960-

Edward
1964-

David
Viscount Linley
1961-

Sarah
1964-

David
Viscount
Lascelles
1950-

James
1953-

Robert
1955-

Peter
1977-

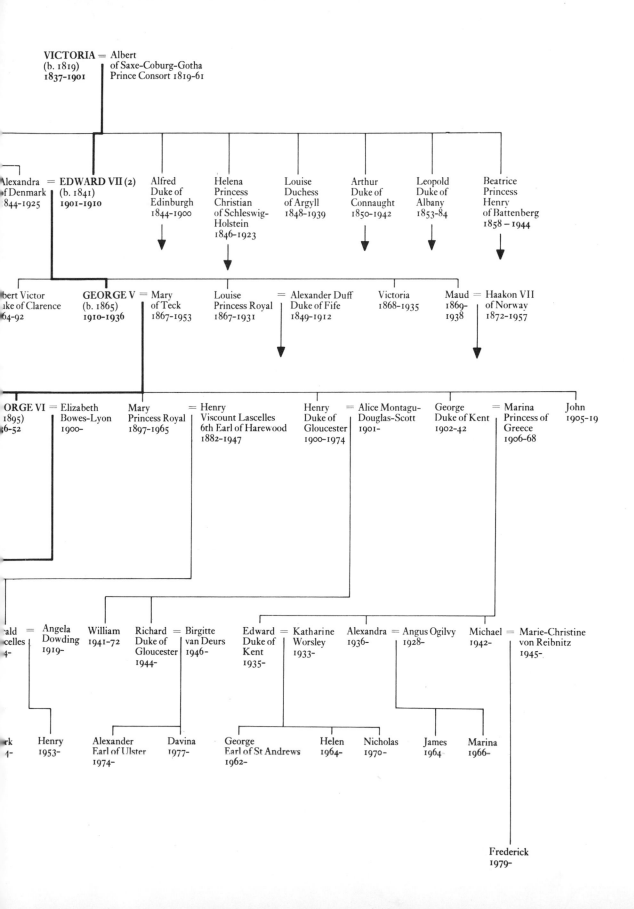

VICTORIA = Albert
(b. 1819) of Saxe-Coburg-Gotha
1837-1901 Prince Consort 1819-61

Alexandra = **EDWARD VII (2)**   Alfred   Helena   Louise   Arthur   Leopold   Beatrice
of Denmark   (b. 1841)   Duke of   Princess   Duchess   Duke of   Duke of   Princess
844-1925   1901-1910   Edinburgh   Christian   of Argyll   Connaught   Albany   Henry
                                 1844-1900   of Schleswig-   1848-1939   1850-1942   1853-84   of Battenberg
                                                  Holstein   1858 – 1944
                                                  1846-1923

bert Victor   **GEORGE V** = Mary   Louise   = Alexander Duff   Victoria   Maud   = Haakon VII
ike of Clarence   (b. 1865)   of Teck   Princess Royal   Duke of Fife   1868-1935   1869-   of Norway
64-92   1910-1936   1867-1953   1867-1931   1849-1912   1938   1872-1957

ORGE VI = Elizabeth   Mary   = Henry   Henry   = Alice Montagu-   George   = Marina   John
1895)   Bowes-Lyon   Princess Royal   Viscount Lascelles Duke of   Douglas-Scott   Duke of Kent   Princess of   1905-19
6-52   1900-   1897-1965   6th Earl of Harewood Gloucester   1901-   1902-42   Greece
                                         1882-1947   1900-1974   1906-68

ald = Angela   William   Richard   = Birgitte   Edward   = Katharine   Alexandra = Angus Ogilvy   Michael = Marie-Christine
celles Dowding   1941-72   Duke of   van Deurs   Duke of   Worsley   1936-   1928-   1942-   von Reibnitz
4-   1919-   Gloucester   1946-   Kent   1933-   1945-
                               1944-   1935-

rk   Henry   Alexander   Davina   George   Helen   Nicholas   James   Marina
4-   1953-   Earl of Ulster 1977-   Earl of St Andrews 1964-   1970-   1964   1966-
                   1974-   1962-

                                                                                                           Frederick
                                                                                                           1979-

Acknowledgments

Photographs and illustrations are supplied or are reproduced by kind permission of the following:

The pictures on pages *4* right, *20*, *23*, *37*, *67* are reproduced by gracious permission of H.M. the Queen.

Godfrey Argent: 114
Associated Newspaper Group Ltd: *108*
Courtesy of Sir Cecil Beaton: *36*, *84* above and below
Camera Press: *3* centre and *4* left (Marcus Adams), 6 (Les Wilson), 9 (Patrick Lichfield), *30* (Marcus Adams), *50* above, 54 (Karsh of Ottawa), *68* below (Marcus Adams), 79, 83 & 101 (Baron), 106, 111, 114 above & 118–19 (Patrick Lichfield), 120 (R. Slade), 121, 125 above (Les Wilson), 130 (Arthur Edwards), 136, 142 (Sir Cecil Beaton), 144 below left, 145 (Andrew Davidson), 158 (Oliver Strewe), 161 above left and right, 163 above (Henry Peplow), 166 above (Tim Graham), 169 left (Patrick Lichfield), 171 below, 173 & 176 (Patrick Lichfield)
Central Press: 133, 146 below
Colour Library International: 123, 134, 139
Cooper-Bridgeman Library: 40–1
Express Newspapers Ltd: *170* left
Fox Photos London: 26, 45, *52*, *58*, *60–1*, *62*, 68 above, 74, 87, *91* above, 98 above, 99 below, 109, 112, 116, 126, 131 below, 132, 160 right, 162 above left, 174
John Frost Historical Newspapers Service: *53*
Anwar Hussein: 144 above, centre and below centre
Illustrated London News: 73 above, centre and below

Serge Lemoine: 144 centre left and below right
National Maritime Museum: 8 centre left (detail)
National Portrait Gallery: 8 above left and right, centre right, below left and right (details)
Popperfoto: 2, 5 centre, 10, 13, 14, *16* above and below, *21*, 25, *34*, *39*, *43* above and below, 46, *50* centre and below, 57 below, 65, 77, *82*, 85, 86, 88 90 above and below, *91* below, *93* below, 96 right, 97 above and below, *102*, 112 left and right, 113 above and below, 117, 137, 152, 165 below, 171 above right
Press Association: 1, 110, 115 above, 125 below, *131* above, 135, 140 below, 146 above and centre, 148, 150, 154 (Ron Bell), 157, 159, 162 below, 163 below, 165 above, 166 centre left, centre right, and below (Ron Bell), 168 left (Ron Bell) and right, *169* right, 171 far right
Radio Times Hulton Picture Library: 64
Rex Features: *32*, *70*, *71*, *170* right
The Sun Newspaper: *138*
Syndication International: *81*, *128*, *149*, *151*, *160* below
Topix: *93* above
Stuart Windsor: Endpapers

The stamps on page 96 and bank notes on page 140 were photographed by kind permission of Stanley Gibbons Ltd. The Coronation and Jubilee memorabilia on pages 98 and 161 were loaned by kind permission of Andrew Kay. Picture research by Lucy Shankleman.

Numbers in italic indicate black and white illustrations.

Index

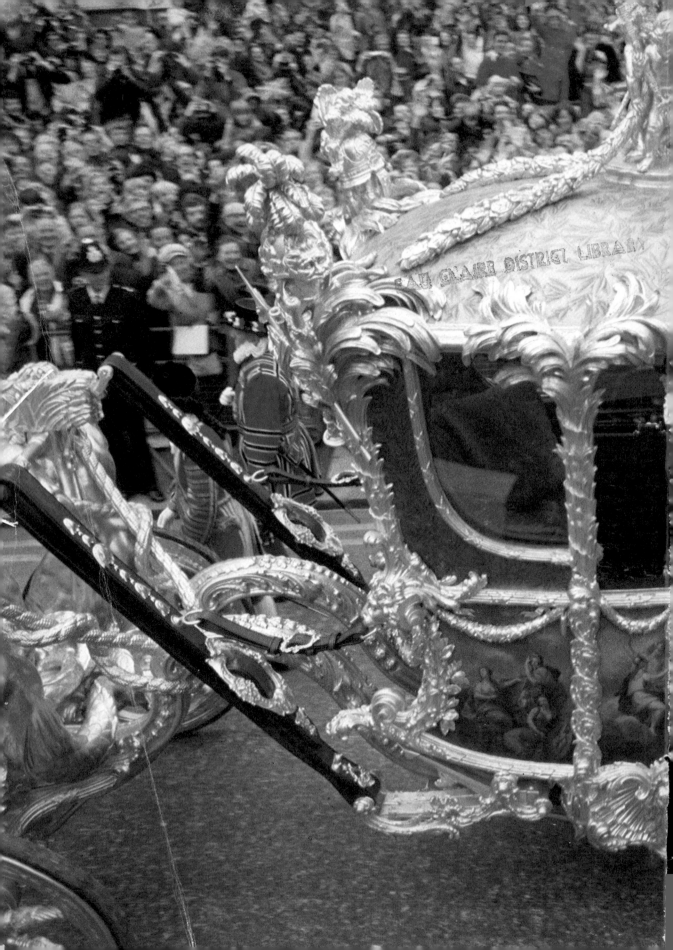